Praise for *Joining a Nonprofit Board*

"This book is a useful road map for the successful businessperson who now wants to 'give back to society' by serving on a nonprofit board and unwittingly assumes that the approaches that worked so well in the for-profit world can be seamlessly extrapolated to the nonprofit board room."

—Roseanna H. Means, M.D., founder and president,
Women of Means

"This book is a must-read for all new nonprofit board members (and existing nonprofit board members as well). It is full of practical advice that will help improve the effectiveness of nonprofit board members and the organizations they serve."

—Roger Servison, president emeritus, Boston Museum of Fine Arts, and vice chairman, Boston Symphony Orchestra

"What a powerful new tool now available for anyone involved with governance of America's unique nonprofit enterprises. The analysis is cogent and concise, amply supported by real life examples."

—George B. Beitzel, chairman emeritus, Amherst College, and chairman emeritus, Colonial Williamsburg Foundation

"This book gives you practical advice in complementing your business experience with the nuances of not-for-profit governance, performance management, and other areas in fully achieving the societal mission."

—Jeffrey C. Thomson, president and CEO,
Institute of Management Accountants

"This book is a must-read for all prospective board members of nonprofit organizations. It guides you through the very real differences between for-profit and nonprofit organizations (and boards). Even more important, it helps one navigate through all the nuances in which nonprofit organizations actually operate on a day-to-day basis."

—Elaine Ullian, former president, Boston Medical Center

"Both for trustees new to nonprofit board work and those who are currently serving, *Joining a Nonprofit Board* is a must read. I would recommend that *Joining a Nonprofit Board* be required reading and distributed at the opening board meeting."

—Agnes C. Underwood, former head, Garrison Forest School and National Cathedral School; vice president/ managing associate, Carney, Sandoe, and Associates

"A board needs a unifying and visionary objective —'It must be world class.' This book successfully shows how to create a world-class board."

—W. Richard Bingham, former chairman, California Academy of Sciences

Joining a Nonprofit Board

Joining a Nonprofit Board

What You Need to Know

Marc J. Epstein
Rice University

F. Warren McFarlan
Harvard Business School

Foreword by Gail McGovern

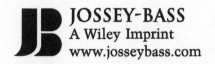

JOSSEY-BASS
A Wiley Imprint
www.josseybass.com

Published by Jossey-Bass
A Wiley Imprint
989 Market Street, San Francisco, CA 94103-1741—www.josseybass.com

Jossey-Bass books and products are available through most bookstores. To contact Jossey-Bass directly call our Customer Care Department within the U.S. at 800-956-7739, outside the U.S. at 317-572-3986, or fax 317-572-4002.

Jossey-Bass also publishes its books in a variety of electronic formats. Some content that appears in print may not be available in electronic books.

Library of Congress Cataloging-in-Publication Data
Epstein, Marc J.
  Joining a nonprofit board : what you need to know / Marc J. Epstein, F. Warren McFarlan ; foreword by Gail McGovern. — 1st ed.
      p. cm.
  Includes bibliographical references and index.
  ISBN 978-0-470-93125-7 (cloth)
  1. Nonprofit organizations—Management. 2. Boards of directors. I. McFarlan, F. Warren II. Title.
  HD62.6.E67 2011
  658.4'22—dc22

Printed in the United States of America
FIRST EDITION
HB Printing V10002078_070718

Contents

Exhibits, Figures, and Tables

Foreword

More and more, businesses are looking to contribute to the greater welfare of society through corporate social responsibility initiatives. Similarly, I have a noticed a trend in business leaders looking to give back on an individual level through service on a nonprofit board. This is a wonderful and rewarding form of volunteerism, but as I have learned, there are significant distinctions between for-profit and nonprofit board service. Luckily, Marc Epstein and Warren McFarlan offer an in-depth synthesis of helpful information to guide individuals on their journey of nonprofit board service with *Joining a Nonprofit Board: What You Need to Know*.

There is no doubt that business leaders have much to offer in terms of expertise to a nonprofit board. Nonprofits must be financially stable, yet this is often one of the greatest challenges to a nonprofit. As financial oversight is a key function of the board, experienced executives can lend valuable financial skills that can help the organization improve efficiencies and thrive. However, as *Joining a Nonprofit Board: What You Need to Know* reveals, board members must understand that the role of finance will vary in a nonprofit organization, and therefore they must be sensitive to the different nuances in financial reporting.

As most nonprofits rely heavily on philanthropy for major financial support, board members are expected to serve another important role, that of philanthropist and fundraiser. Not only are nonprofit board members not compensated for their service on the board, they are also expected to contribute financially to the organization. Again, the authors provide valuable guidance on this aspect of service, encouraging individuals to seek clarity on these expectations before joining the board.

In addition to personal contributions, board members will also be active in cultivating donors and raising funds through direct solicitation. Board members serve as key ambassadors, deepening existing relationships and fostering new relationships on behalf of the organization. This can require travel and a considerable amount of time. Furthermore, your commitment to the organization may extend beyond just your term on the board. Involvement can sometimes be for life, as former board members will be called upon to participate in various ways and contribute financially.

In my experience with nonprofits, I have been inspired by the manner in which the mission is the motivating force of the organization. Employees are often driven by the fulfillment of the mission and not necessarily monetary gain. Your fellow board members, too, are likely to be personally invested and passionate about the work they are doing. As a result, when suggesting change, it is even more important to earn trust, build consensus, and move forward together as an organization. I have found that this provides opportunities to develop strong relationships with fellow board members, as you work together to achieve the shared mission.

Furthermore, because profits are not the bottom line, it can be difficult to monitor progress and gauge overall success of a nonprofit organization and its employees. Chapter Three lays out an important methodology for measuring nonfinancial performance which all nonprofit board members should consider, as they concurrently evaluate whether the mission is being carried out in a fiscally responsible manner.

Given the significant participation that is expected, it is essential for individuals to fully understand and believe in the mission of the organization before deciding to serve. The requirements may be substantial, but in giving of my time, talent, and resources, I have found that I am personally invested in the organization and even more moved to ensure its success. As a result, my service on nonprofit boards has been extremely rewarding.

However, passion alone is not enough. As you will come to understand in reading this book, it is important to ensure that you have the time and the energy to be an active and valuable contributor; otherwise, neither you nor the organization stand to gain.

When I joined my first nonprofit board eighteen years ago, I was not fully aware of all that was expected of me in this role. As a business executive, I knew I had much to contribute from my professional experience; however, no one had told me about the time and resources which were also an essential part of my service as a nonprofit board member. There were so many questions I should have asked when starting out, yet to my knowledge there was no comprehensive guide available to help prepare me for this responsibility.

As an individual who has served on various nonprofit boards, and as the president and CEO of a large nonprofit organization, I can attest to how valuable this book is. Marc Epstein and Warren McFarlan offer insight into the expectations of nonprofit board members, which is extraordinarily beneficial to individuals considering their first nonprofit board and to seasoned professionals already serving on boards. This book will allow you to be a stronger contributor, preparing you with questions to ask when deciding whether or not to join, and continuing to guide you once you are a board member. Needless to say, I wish this book had existed when I started on my first nonprofit board, but there is no doubt that this guide will be an important resource as I continue my service. I know you will agree.

—Gail McGovern
President and CEO, American Red Cross

Preface

We have spent much of our professional careers working with nonprofit organization boards. Sometimes it has been as a researcher, consultant, writer, adviser, or teacher. Sometimes it has been as an active member or chair of a board of trustees. The nonprofits that we have worked with have ranged from small to large, local to global, and are located in developing and developed countries. Some have been social impact focused and others member focused. But the questions that all posed to us are unusually similar. How do I improve performance in these surprisingly complex organizations?

We have also served for over three decades on privately and publicly traded corporate boards, heavily but not exclusively located in the United States. We have been deeply struck by not just the similarities but by the differences between the rhythms in the for-profit board processes and structures and those of their nonprofit counterparts. Although there has been convergence over the past two decades, the reality is that the differences between nonprofit boards and corporate boards are both profound and deep.

Our careers have been based at business schools. And though we have extensive work with nonprofits, we have often viewed their challenges through the lens of business professionals surprised that they cannot easily take their business knowledge and experience and transport it seamlessly to the nonprofit sector. Though this book is written for both new and experienced nonprofit board members, it is particularly focused on those with a business background and mindset who serve or are about to serve on a nonprofit board. Though there are many similarities to business, there are also significant differences— differences so significant that if you are not consciously address- ing the differences, your nonprofit service will be frustrating— both for you and the organization. And your service will not be as beneficial as it can be—either for you or the organization!

You are likely to join a nonprofit board because you care about the mission. The mission is primary, and don't ever lose focus on that. The finances are also important because non- profits cannot thrive unless they are financially sustainable. This book addresses the many questions that we are often asked. But, at its core, the questions pertain to: (a) achieving mission; (b) achieving financial sustainability; and (c) developing and executing the systems to accomplish both. This book is about the role of nonprofit boards in improving the success of non- profit organizations. And it is about how individuals with suc- cessful business experience can appreciate the differences that nonprofits have and can leverage their business experience to make a major contribution.

We start with the mission and measuring performance against it, as that must be the primary focus. But financial skills are criti- cal to provide and manage the resources to accomplish the mission. We then examine the special nonprofit board challenges of size, skills, composition, types of committees, philanthropy, the relationship of a nonexecutive board chair to the CEO, and so on, all of which are very different in the nonprofit world.

It is this necessity to achieve success at both mission and finances that make nonprofit management especially challeng- ing. Too many nonprofits fail at one or both of these. To achieve excellence in nonprofit boards—whether social impact focused or member focused—success on mission, finances, and execution are all critical.

This book is written for individuals with a for-profit back- ground, or with understanding of a for-profit business, who are joining their first nonprofit board. We believe it will also be useful for experienced board members, who sometimes can lose track of the big picture in the press of operational business. We highlight how different the roles and activities are on a nonprofit board. This book is also directed at nonprofit leaders, with the goal of helping them to understand the very different perspective that their board members from the for-profit world bring to their organizations.

At the center of the book (Figure P.1) are the roles and responsibilities of the board. These are laid out in summary form in Chapter One. The heart of the nonprofit board's role is the *building and monitoring of mission*, its very reason for existence. Mission, given the lack of a profit and loss statement, is especially important in the nonprofit world and is elaborated on in Chapter Two. Chapter Three identifies how the board does *performance assessment of the organization*. This is a complex and important task as surrogate measures are identified to replace profit and loss measures. Chapters Four and Five focus on the board's role in *securing and monitoring finances* for the organization. Philanthropy is such an important aspect of nonprofit finance that an entire chapter is devoted to the issues related to its securing.

Figure P.1 Book Organization

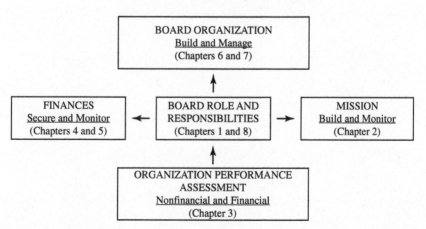

Chapters Six and Seven define the issues and challenges in *organizing and managing* the nonprofit board with its large size (in many cases) and plethora of committees. Special attention in Chapter Seven is given to the challenges posed by the duality of leadership in most nonprofits between the unpaid volunteer, nonexecutive chairman of the board and the paid CEO. This role separation is different from how things are done in many U.S. for-profit organizations. Finally, Chapter Eight traces through a life cycle as a trustee, beginning with the issues involved in deciding whether you should join the board. It then successively covers how to prepare for your first meeting, how to effectively use your first two years on the board, your ongoing and developing role as a trustee, and finally your transition off the board to other forms of engagement with the organization.

Acknowledgments

The material in this book is the outgrowth of field research done over the past decade at Rice University and Harvard Business School (HBS), and over thirty years of active nonprofit and for-profit board service by the authors. We are particularly grateful to Dean John McArthur at Harvard Business School who launched this work and Harvard Business School Deans Kim Clark and Jay Light and Rice Dean Bill Glick who have supported it over a number of years.

We are indebted to all the board members and nonprofit executives we have worked with over the years. All the examples in the book come from real organizations and are the result of observations of strategic decisions and actions. Some organizations we are able to publicly thank, such as Trinity College, Mt. Auburn Hospital, Dana Hall School, and Opportunity International. Others must remain anonymous.

A special note of thanks is due to Professor Emeritus Jim Austin at Harvard Business School who launched the Social Enterprise effort at HBS nearly fifteen years ago and brought us together, and to John Whitehead, former chair of Goldman Sachs and for many years chairman of the HBS Social Enterprise Advisory Committee, who facilitated the whole effort.

Our special thanks go to our spouses who supported us through thousands of hours away from home at nonprofit board meetings. Fortunately there was almost always shared familial belief in the importance of the mission of nonprofits we worked with.

Our colleagues Dutch Leonard, Kash Rangan, Mark Moore, Alnoor Ebrahim, and Jane Wei Skillern have been very supportive, as has been Laura Moon, director of the HBS Social Enterprise effort. Special thanks go to our colleagues Alan Grossman and Jay Lorsch for their insightful feedback on earlier drafts and to our editors Allison Brunner and Kathe Sweeney for their many helpful contributions. The final responsibility for what appears in the book is ours. Finally, we are grateful to Paula   Alexander, Maureen Donovan, Janice Simmons, Luz Velazquez, and Margaret de Sosa for their invaluable administrative support.

This book is dedicated to
Professor James E. Austin
and
John C. Whitehead,
Social Enterprise Pioneers

1

INTRODUCTION

Congratulations on having joined the board of a nonprofit! You have just become part of one of the most fulfilling and personally satisfying sectors of the economy. Currently, nonprofits account for more than 10 percent of the United States' economic activity and employment. Nonprofits cover a wide array of organizations spanning hospitals (half of which are nonprofits), schools, colleges, museums, professional service organizations, social service organizations, and so on. The boards of all of these organizations are rooted deeply in the American tradition of volunteerism and trying to help others. You are unpaid and giving of yourself to the community.

The number of nonprofit organizations has increased dramatically in recent years. These include a wide variety of organizations from charitable organizations, social services, religious and fraternal organizations, health care societies and health organizations, educational organizations, environmental organizations, sports and recreational organizations, to funding foundations, business and professional organizations, political parties, and so on. Their purpose is to generate improvements in the lives of individuals, members, organizations, communities, and society as a whole. Some of these organizations, such as charities, may be considered purely *social impact focused*, whereas others, such as professional organizations, may be primarily viewed as *member focused*. However, classifying nonprofit organizations is not easy as some have elements of both types. For this reason, one should rather think of a continuum of nonprofit organizations spanning

Table 1.1 Structure of Organizations

Usually Nonprofits	May Be For-Profit or Nonprofit	For-Profit
Charitable	Educational institutions	Publicly traded corporations
Professional associations	Hospitals	Privately held firms
Religious and fraternal organizations		
Environmental		
Community foundations		

from purely socially focused to purely member focused organizations with numerous nonprofit organizations having dual roles of serving both their members and society. And, as noted in Table 1.1, there are some types of organizations that are always organized as nonprofits, whereas others like hospitals and certain educational institutions may be either for-profits or nonprofits.

Participation in nonprofits is a very important part of business executives' lives and until relatively recently unrecognized. Business leaders find themselves on boards of directors of nonprofit organizations. We also find these organizations being led by professionals from the business world including professional accountants instead of individuals from traditional social service backgrounds. Surveys of HBS alumni for example show 80 percent or more self-report being involved with nonprofits during their careers with more than 50 percent serving or having served on one or more nonprofit boards. These organizations vary in size from small community music schools to multibillion dollar health organizations. These activities are widely supported by American culture (despite description in such books as *Bowling Alone: The Collapse and Revival of American Community*[1]) and by U.S. federal tax policy where the Internal Revenue Service gives substantial relief for charitable deductions. In addition, local communities often exempt assets of nonprofits from taxes (although in Massachusetts, for example, colleges and hospitals often give gifts to the towns and cities in lieu of taxes).

The roots of philanthropy go well back into the nineteenth century. Names of great business leaders like Andrew Carnegie, J. P. Morgan, and John D. Rockefeller spring quickly to mind, as also being enormously significant philanthropists. Warren Buffet and Bill and Melinda Gates are present-day philanthropists whose work attracts our attention.

We find the topic remains relevant to the leaders of tomorrow, with today's MBA students showing especial interest. Nearly half of the MBA students at the Harvard Business School are currently enrolled in one or more nonprofit courses, with nearly 10 percent of the incoming class coming from this sector as full-time employees. These facts have held for the past five years. On graduation, 3–5 percent of the class takes internships or appointments in the sector. Indeed, this phenomena is a global one with significant numbers of nonprofit CEOs (throughout the book the terms CEO, *president*, and *executive director* will be used synonymously) coming to Harvard's nonprofit programs from as far as Australia, China, Singapore, India, and the United Kingdom. This book, however, will be primarily focused on the United States because of its very large role as a matter of public policy (which cedes to nonprofits significant domains that are covered by government in other countries). The United States also has a strong focus on individual philanthropy that is quite unique in the world.

Comparing Nonprofits and For-Profits

There are a number of important similarities and differences between the operations and challenges of nonprofits and for-profits of which a new nonprofit board member must be cognizant. Some of the more important items are discussed in this section.

Similarities

There are a number of similarities between for-profits and non-profits which make people with for-profit experience particularly helpful as board members. The key similarities include:

1. Both organizations can grow, transform, merge, or die. Success is not guaranteed for either type of organization, but requires sustained work.
2. In both cases, cash is king. This for-profit focus is critical for a nonprofit board.
3. In both settings, good management and leadership really matter. Delivery of service, motivating and inspiring staff, and conceiving of new directions for growth are all vitally important.
4. Planning, budgeting, and performance measurement systems are vital in both settings.
5. Both types of organizations face the challenges of integrating subject matter specialists into a generalist framework.
6. Both organizations add value to society. They just do it in different ways.

In short, there is much overlap between the skills needed and perspectives provided by leaders in the two types of organizations. This is a key reason why social enterprise courses have taken root in business schools and why, appropriately socialized, those with for-profit backgrounds can contribute so much to the nonprofit world.

Having noted all of this, the blunt question in your mind is: why do I need to read a book on nonprofit management? Isn't it just a subset of the for-profit world, with little difference in the tasks and perspectives of managers and board members? Cannot the tools, practices, and viewpoints developed through a career of successful for-profit work be transferred to this new realm of nonprofit? The authors answer this question with an emphatic no! Although, as noted, many aspects are the same, in important areas there are deep differences. Failure to understand these differences can cause the new board member to stumble badly and perhaps irretrievably damage her credibility and effectiveness in a nonprofit organization.

Differences

At its core the nonprofit is fundamentally different than the for-profit. At the center of the nonprofit is its societal mission. Understanding the mission, helping the organization to fulfill it, and adapting it to a changing world is the very core of nonprofit governance and management. It is for this reason this book starts with a detailed discussion of mission and how it grows. Without the mission there is no purpose. Right behind this are the two major intertwined strategic themes that the nonprofit trustee must deal with.

The first theme is fulfilling the mission and whether we are doing it in a fiscally responsible fashion. Chapter Two deals with the complex multifaceted issue of mission definition and evaluation of its appropriateness. Chapter Three shows, in a series of examples, how organizations can go about measuring their performance against mission. For the new trustee, understanding these issues is the place to begin her trusteeship. The second theme is financial solvency. Chapter Four deals with the board's fiduciary responsibility and financial sustainability. Our life experience drives us to put this behind "performance measurement against mission." Repeatedly we have seen new trustees and ineffective boards try to wag the mission dog with the financial tail. It just doesn't work that way. Without mission and its accountability we have nothing.

Achieving financial sustainability is very different for the nonprofit than the for-profit in that the nonprofit cannot easily access the public equity markets but instead has philanthropy as a potential additional source of funds. Chapter Five deals with the role of philanthropy and the trustee's role in it. This may be summarized by giving often and generously and when not giving helping others to give (hence the phrase give, get, or get off).

Finally, the execution of the work of the board is deeply different from that of boards in the for-profit world because of the tasks of mission performance measurement and different capital markets. As Chapter Six describes in detail, nonprofit boards are often larger, have more committees, and have a very different trustee life cycle. Further, as Chapter Seven describes, the heart of the governance process is a volunteer nonexecutive chairman and volunteer board, leading a staff of paid professionals. The dynamics of this are complex and profoundly different from the process in the for-profit world. Chapter Eight returns directly to you, the new trustee, addressing what you should consider before deciding to join a board and what you can do to make your trusteeship personally beneficial to you and the organization. The rest of this chapter gives an overview of these differences, which provide the structure of the book. These are highlighted in Table 1.2.

I. Mission

In the absence of the discipline of a P&L statement, the development of a mission and measuring progress against it is a critical and different nonprofit task. Neither developing the mission nor tracking progress against it is easy to do. Mission will be discussed extensively in Chapter Two and mission performance metrics in Chapter Three, but we present a brief overview here. As a new trustee your single most important task in the first year is to internalize the full breadth and complexity of the organization's mission and assess how well you think the organization is working toward achieving it.

In the for-profit world, an economist would argue that the main objective and mission of an organization is through the provision of goods and services to earn an appropriate return on

Table 1.2 Key Differences of For-Profit Versus Nonprofit Governance

For-Profits	Nonprofits
Mission	
Mission important	Mission very important
Financial results	Cash loss generator may be key service
Nonfinancial metrics important	Nonfinancial metrics of mission performance very important
Finance	
Financial metrics of performance P&L, stock price, and cash flow very important	Financial metrics of meeting budget and cash flow projections also important
Funds come from operations and financial capital markets	Funds come from operations, debt, grants, and philanthropy
Short-term goals very important	Deep focus on long-term goals (as long as cash is there)
Executive	
Small board—paid governance	Often large board—volunteer governance
Few board committees	Often many board committees
Combined chair/CEO plus lead director	Nonexecutive volunteer chair, plus CEO

invested capital for its shareholders. The organization, of course, provides an additional variety of ancillary services such as employment, tax support for the community and state, and special contributions to local communities.

The nonprofit operates in the space between government-provided services and for-profit ones. Absent the discipline of the financial market on the one hand and government mandate on the other hand, special clarity is needed to both effectively allocate financial resources and monitor how they are spent. These tasks bring us to mission and mission accountability.

In its most basic form, mission is the reason the organization exists. It defines the specific social services the organization provides, guides investment decisions, and provides a basis for its performance to be evaluated. A case in point is the mission statement of the Dana Hall School,[2] a 100-year-old girls' school, which evolved through twenty-six drafts in a time of financial stress. In part, the statement reads: "Dana Hall School is committed to fostering excellence in academics, the arts and athletics within a vibrant caring community. . . . [It] provides its students with a unique opportunity to prepare themselves for challenges and choices as women."

The ideas in here were powerful. First, it will remain an all-girls' school because of the unique contribution it can make to *women*. Supported by a lot of research, it was nonetheless an out-of-favor concept at the time the mission statement was developed, in the mid-1980s. Leadership as well as math and science capabilities are examples of skills that research shows can be increased by all-girls' education. Secondly, it will strive to be excellent in academics ("We are not a remedial school and academics is our first priority"). Right behind (but behind) are arts and athletics, both of which can be very capital intensive. Next the word "caring" leaps out. "We are not Darwinian in our culture, but seek to help and be supportive." It can be contrasted with the mission statement of its closest competitor (a very fast-track all-girls' school, over half of whose graduates go to the Ivy League): "dedicated to developing the individual talents of academically promising and motivated girls." Finally, we can look at the statement of a boys' school in the same area: "dedicated to developing boys in mind, body and spirit . . . challeng[ing] and support[ing] students in and beyond the classroom . . . honor[ing] clear thinking and creativity, competition and team work. . . ." Not surprisingly, this all-boys' school has very strong athletic teams and good students.

Each of these statements captures the essence of a very different set of values—all good, but very different. For Dana Hall in 1995, following a decade of heavy operating losses, confidence in this mission meant taking on $8 million in debt to build a new world-class science center; several years later it took on more debt and built a world-class athletic center. Science, women, and excellence all combined to make this the obvious first investment and worth undertaking the attendant financial risk in a stretched organization. In 2010 it is thriving academically as it still deals with its debt load. In discussing mission numerous additional points emerge that are elaborated on in Chapter Two.

Mission Development Process. The process of developing and disseminating mission is as important as the mission itself. The power of the Dana Hall Mission stemmed from a six-month series of discussions. These meetings included spirited discussions within the board, parents, alumni, student body, and faculty. Out of these discussions came a shared sense of strategic alignment and deep personal commitment "to take the path less travelled" which was crucial for an organization facing a time of financial stress. Finally it should be noted that because board membership changes over time, that the mission needs to be periodically revisited in discussions so that new members can be informed and feel informed.

II. Nonfinancial Performance Metrics Against Mission

Over the past fifteen years, corporations have increasingly recognized the importance of appropriate nonfinancial performance metrics in evaluating organizational success in addition to the more traditional financial metrics (see for example, work on the balanced scorecard or dashboard). These measures of performance are desperately needed by most nonprofit organizations. What are the relevant indicators of performance?

Today many nonprofit organizations have been developing new performance measurement models and performance measures to track their nonfinancial performance. One example of a social impact–focused organization that has made progress here is KaBOOM! An example of a member-focused nonprofit organization that has made progress here is CMA Canada. More examples of measurement systems that can be used to evaluate performance against mission will be discussed in Chapter Three.

KaBOOM! is a nonprofit organization with the mission of building playgrounds and creating safe places to play for children all over America and a related goal of inspiring local residents to work together and become more proactive in revitalizing and maintaining their communities.[3] The organization has created an overall performance measurement system which includes the following financial performance measures: build efficiency in cost per build (actual versus planned), program efficiency (program expenses as percentage of total expenses), fund-raising efficiency (dollars spent to generate one dollar in revenue). Other indicators include total cash available at the end of the period, burn rate per month, annual revenue growth, total annual budget, and funds raised toward budget.

Along with these efficiency performance measures, KaBOOM! board uses other performance indicators to assess past impacts and to steer the organization toward future success. Exhibit 1.1 illustrates some of these other performance indicators.

CMA Canada, responsible for standards setting, accreditation, and the continuing professional development of Certified Management Accountants (CMAs), has a mission, "CMA drives value creation by developing professionals and resources to lead the advancement and integration of strategy, accounting and management," and a vision, "CMA is the designation of choice." The CMA Canada National Board of Directors and the Council of Chairs who is monitoring the twelve provincial and territorial partners and the national partner recognized the importance of measuring the progress of the initiatives in the strategic plan. A *multijurisdictional* balanced scorecard was therefore developed to measure the progress of the initiatives for CMA Canada, as well as the collective initiatives of all

Exhibit 1.1. Sample: KaBOOM! Performance Indicator[4]

Performance measures

- Total number of volunteers per year
- Average number of volunteers per build
- Organizational culture
  - Staff turnover rate (gross)
  - Culture rating (scale from 1 to 4)
- Brand
  - Number of media mentions per year
  - Number of click-throughs per year
  - Number of target marketing mentions per year
- Number of children served within walking distance (actual versus plan)
- Number of new or renewed playful sites
- Number of playgrounds built; started and completed
- Number of individuals who have taken a step beyond volunteering on a build

---

partners. Figure 1.1 presents an overview of the CMA Canada's balanced scorecard, its central vision and strategy, perspectives, and the related major success factors.

The "learning and growth perspective" is considered the most important one in the model, as it fuels the stakeholder and internal business processes. The partners of CMA Canada have implemented a number of initiatives designed to increase the amount and effectiveness of this perspective. Each staff member also has a *personal balanced scorecard* and is rewarded after achieving the measures. The employees have thus been provided with a greater learning focus that is directly related to the strategic objectives of

Figure 1.1 CMA Canada Balanced Scorecard[5]

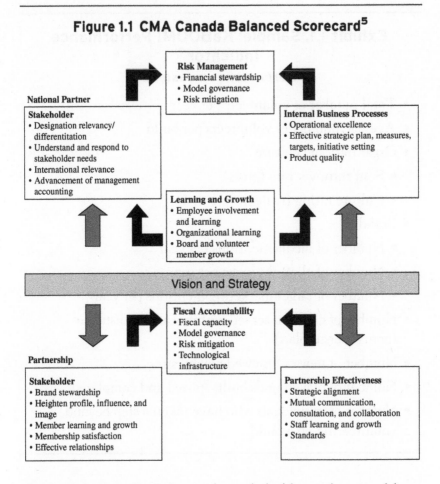

the organization. To achieve the stakeholder and internal business process objectives, volunteers, especially the governance of the organization, also have established learning objectives in order to ensure that their fiduciary responsibilities are being effectively carried out. The strength of the volunteer learning objective is that the governance of the CMA partners is more focused on the strategic direction of the CMA partnership.[6]

III. Financial Metrics

The financial metrics and incentives are dramatically different between the two worlds. The income statement, earnings per share, and growth in market capitalization are all widely focused performance metrics and important components of long-term and short-term executive performance assessment and compensation in the for-profit world. There are literally no analogies for these items in the nonprofit world. There is no ritual of tracking one's stock price on a continuous basis on PC screens in the nonprofit world. Two financial metrics of the for-profit world, free cash flow and revenue growth, however, are very relevant to the nonprofit world. As will be described in Chapter Five, an important additional source of funds for the nonprofit world is philanthropy in its various forms of annual giving, capital campaigns, and planned giving. The accounting framework for nonprofits is very different from that of for-profits. As will be noted in Chapter Four, normal accrual accounting concepts are often not applied, and something called "fund accounting" is used instead. Depreciation is often not used and fixed assets may be stated at a fraction of their real value. Informality of accounting practice may lead to the creation of very significant off–balance sheet liabilities. For those organizations that have an endowment, significant pressures exist on the board to both effectively manage it and have an appropriate rate of withdrawal. Cash flow is king with annual giving and capital gifts often being critical to financial viability. Finally, debt and its servicing status are important issues for those nonprofits that have access to the public debt market.

In short, there is need for for-profit financial skills on the nonprofit board, but the individuals have to be very sensitive to both the different nuances in financial reporting and to the role of finance in the nonprofit. This second point is particularly true because trustees who come from a for-profit background tend to relate well to the chief financial officer (CFO). That individual is often the only one in the nonprofit who speaks a language close to theirs. Conversely, the CFO, often frustrated by the problems of "mission-related" issues getting in the way of financial prudence, is delighted to find a kindred soul in the new board member. Whenever possible, we recommend trying to keep the new trustee off the finance committee for the first year or two and instead assign him or her to a mission-related committee to absorb the values and purposes of the organization before getting involved in the cost/service tradeoffs that the Finance Committee must make. Obviously, this cautionary note does not apply to membership on the audit and investment committees whose activities are much more independent of mission.

Because of the metrics of financial reporting, the for-profit world tends to have a strong short-term performance focus. Meeting the quarterly earnings targets, the annual earnings goal, and the steady drumbeat of the stock price all drive a short-term orientation. To overcome this, a variety of mid- and long-term incentive and planning tools have been put in place in the for-profit world to try to lengthen managerial horizons and focus on strategic challenges. Repeatedly, however, these approaches can be undercut after a three-hour strategy session, when the CEO asks in a throwaway comment what this means to next quarter's earnings. The very question in that setting dampens incentive for strategic thinking.

The pace of the nonprofit could not be more different. The heart of its financial activities is the preparation of the annual budget, its forecast of revenues, and the hard choices that are made on various costs. Monthly reviews focus on success in meeting cost and revenue targets where variances against budget are repeatedly analyzed. As will be discussed in Chapter Three, this is often complemented by a balanced scorecard or dashboard approach. The reality, however, is that negative variances just do not have the same impact on internal and external perceptions of performance as a missed EPS number does for the for-profit. Beyond all of this, of course, is the need to peer around the corner and look toward the long-term future challenges to the organization (sometimes five to ten years in the future).

IV. Governance

Best practice in governance has been changing for both profits and nonprofits in the past decade. For the for-profit world these issues have been very high profile. Many of these changes in for-profit governance have had an impact on the world of non-profits. Beyond these changes in common, however, there are very significant differences between nonprofit governance and for-profit governance which are briefly noted here and will be discussed at length later in Chapters Six and Seven.

Best practice in for-profit governance has changed significantly in the past decade as a result of the excesses triggered by WorldCom, Tyco, and Enron. Key changes include:

1. The creation of the position of lead director, who is responsible for board process and direct continuous communication with the CEO. Although there is also significant movement to a nonexecutive chairman, the emergence of the lead director's role has muted some of the concerns on this topic. As will be noted, in nonprofits the unpaid nonexecutive chairman has always been the dominant organizational form.

2. Regularly scheduled executive sessions of external directors only, to create an environment for candid discussion of board concerns, review of CEO performance, and so on. This regular schedule is critical in blurring the organizational anxiety that tends to arise whenever a special executive meeting of external directors is called. This has had an equal impact on nonprofits.

3. An expanded role of the audit committee as a result of Sarbanes-Oxley and the requirement that at least one member must be a "financial expert" (a former CFO, CEO, or accounting firm partner). The average length of the for-profit audit committee meeting has grown by several hundred percent as dealing with material compliance issues

have became a much more important activity. This has become of equal concern to the nonprofit as a result of the new accounting standard for nonprofits, SAS112.

4. In 2011, the role of the compensation committee has become much more burdensome as a result of heightened public and regulatory concern over executive compensation. We are seeing much more use of outside consultants and benchmarking against peer group performance. Additionally, particular care is now taken with regard to the awarding of stock options and its associated accounting. The compensation committee has also become more important for the nonprofit. Excesses in nonprofit compensation have resulted in celebrated cases like Eliot Spitzer's pursuit of Dick Grasso in the New York Stock Exchange, and the attorney general of New Hampshire against the rector of St. Paul's School.

5. The governance committee's role has become more significant. It has taken the initiative of screening and nominating new directors and managing committee assignments (as opposed to an earlier time when the CEO played a much more important role in the process). It also manages the annual CEO evaluation and counseling process (this may be done either by the governance committee or the compensation committee). This is also true for the nonprofit board.

Beyond this list, very different governance processes exist for the nonprofit board that deserve special note. The key ones are discussed in the following sections.

Size

The size of the nonprofit board is larger (sometimes much larger), and its membership is much more heterogeneous. Two factors drive the size. One is the development role of the board.

For some people, an important part of their cultivation is putting them on the board of trustees. This can lead to very large boards of 25 to 30, or even as many as the 130 members who are on the Dana Farber Cancer Institute board (who collectively, with their friends, raise 75 percent of the funds of this most successful fund-raising organization). The second reason for larger size is to have appropriate community representatives who can be the nonprofit's eyes and ears in the community. One third of the board members of a recently studied nonprofit hospital were recruited in this way. They were invaluable as ambassadors in the community and thus indirectly helped to fill beds.

Realistically, these risks of board size are worth bearing because of the benefit of binding certain potential donors closer to the organization. One caveat, however, is that these board members must be able to behave in a discreet way, or at least not to be disruptive of the board processes. One chair of a museum lost the battle of trying to convince the governance committee of the value of appointing someone to the board who had given another organization a major gift, the size of which really caught the attention of the board chair of this cash-starved organization. In no uncertain terms, the governance committee chair would not acquiesce to the appointment as she saw the individual as potentially disruptive to board processes.

Committees

There are often many more committees of the board in the nonprofit than the for-profit. The typical for-profit has an audit committee, a compensation committee, a governance committee, and maybe one other such as public relations or technology. The typical medium-size or larger nonprofit has a variety of standing committees beyond these, including the development committee, investment committee, and facilities committee. These committees are often staffed by individuals of extraordinary talents that the nonprofit could not possibly attract as full-time employees. The large nonprofit is also much more likely to form a series of ad hoc committees to deal with special issues. These could include a CEO search committee, a special program review committee, a capital campaign committee, and so forth.

Volunteer Versus Paid Governance

The motivations of the nonprofit board members and their responsibilities could not be more different from those of their for-profit brethren. For-profit board members are compensated financially well for their service. In addition to attractive retainers and board meeting attendance fees, they are often awarded stock in the company. Former retirement plans have evolved into annual contributions of restricted stock into a deferred compensation plan which only vests on retirement from the board. As a result, they are keenly interested in stock price and the economic performance of the company. There are, to be sure, times of great stress such as hostile takeovers, SEC investigations, and so on. In general, however, board members are well compensated for these events. When they finish their term, or the company is sold, however, the relationship between the director and the company usually abruptly and completely ends. Their participation in a social system disappears.

The world of the nonprofit trustees could not be more different. Not only is there no compensation, but because of the philanthropic aspect the financial compensation is negative and often deeply negative. In some cases, such as museum trusteeship, expectations for capital gifts, annual giving, and participation in galas, and the like are so high that many people cannot afford to consider being a trustee.

Unlike the for-profit board, where time demands are somewhat predictable (other than during a crisis), the longer a trustee remains on a nonprofit board, the more time is demanded until burnout becomes a real problem. Board chairs and chairs of capital campaigns and CEO search committees, for example, are high burnout positions. Recently a board chair of a nonprofit that was six months into a merger was caustically asked by his spouse whether he had quit his regular position (it was actually a fair question based on expenditure of time).

Emotional engagement, however, is one of the real benefits of nonprofit board membership. Though meetings can be long and sometimes meandering, the ability to viscerally contribute to something you believe is really positively changing society is a very powerful tonic and can help you overcome a lot of frustration.

Finally, and most important, unlike the for-profit world, appropriate engagement with a nonprofit is often a lifelong arrangement. When you leave the board, the alert nonprofit makes sure you are involved for the rest of your life. Former trustee meetings, honorary trustees, and membership in the corporation are all tools the nonprofit uses to keep the link for philanthropic and ambassadorial purposes. The reality is the authors have remained in contact with almost all of their former boards and usually contribute financially to them as well.

V. Chair-CEO Relationship

First and foremost, the nonprofit board chair is almost always a volunteer. As will be discussed in Chapter Seven, this is a very important and sensitive relationship, often with significant information asymmetries. In the normal circumstance, the board chair turns over more rapidly than the CEO position. This means the CEO not only has a much deeper grasp (we hope) of the operational nuances but also often a much longer insight into how issues are playing out and their context. Sometimes, however, an incoming chair picked by the governance committee may have a different set of organizational priorities than her predecessor and, in fact, her selection may have been the product of the governance committee wanting to send a signal to the

CEO. Disagreement between the two in public can send confusing signals to all involved. A good friend of the authors chaired three boards. Although she often argued strenuously with the CEOs, she noted that it was always done in private. In public, they were careful to keep a united face so as to not confuse administrators or board members.

While the nonexecutive chair of for-profits is common in the United Kingdom and Australia, it is emerging in the United States. In the nonprofit, the relationship between the chair and the CEO is probably the most important two-person relationship in the organization. As will be discussed in Chapter Seven, it plays out very differently from one organization to another, and evolves over time within an organization. Several preliminary points, however, should be made at this juncture in the book.

1. The governance committee is ultimately responsible for the execution of board governance processes, including those concerning the evaluation and selection of the CEO. This sounds easier than it is because in many nonprofits, the CEO has much longer tenure than the chair and has a much deeper grasp of organization mission and the operational details. Often, in fact, the CEO is such a dominant person in the board meeting that many board members feel like so many docile mushrooms (warm and completely in the dark). Often this works, sometimes even for a long time as shown by the successful forty-year tenure of one New England school head, but when the organization goes off the rails, a heavy burden falls on both the board and the chair to take corrective action.

2. Great care must be taken in selecting the board chair. In times of organizational crisis, the chair will be the person who makes things happen. For example, in 1992 at Trinity College, Connecticut, when both the president and dean resigned, the de facto operational control of the college was

left to the chairman until an interim head was chosen (a one-month period). The chair needs to have the confidence of the board, a good working relationship with the head, and a broad understanding of the organization's mission and operational challenges. This normally means the chair is someone who has spent some time on the board in order to gather these perspectives and develop relationships with the board members. In the spirit of George Orwell, all board members are equal, but some are more equal than others.

3. The CEO is the visible leader of the organization and must be treated in that light. The nonexecutive chair is normally relatively invisible. The CEO is not only the operational leader, but is also the primary external face of the organization. Major prospective donors expect to spend time with the CEO and, in times of capital campaigns, 50 percent or more of the CEO's time is devoted to development. It has been only half facetiously said that a university president is a high-end beggar who lives in a beautiful house.

Shaping and managing the board chair and CEO relationship takes time and effort on both sides. The case of the University of Hawaii board with only a three-year term for all trustees was a recipe for disaster. Going through four chairs in an eighteen-month period several years ago, their lack of experience and organization instability resulted in their firing of the university president in a way that unnecessarily cost the university millions of dollars.

Summary

We hope this quick overview of the nonprofit world excites you and that you will decide to become actively involved in the nonprofit world as a board member. For many, as will be described in Chapter Eight, this is a lifelong relationship. Table 1.3 is a picture of a trustee's life cycle from the beginning of joining a board

Table 1.3   Trustee Life Cycle–Community Services Board Chair

1980–1991	Becomes familiar with organization and contributes to annual fund
1992	Joins the board
1994	Assigned to cochair "alliance task force" following a letter to CEO and chair concerning strategic challenges facing organization
1995–1998	Becomes chair of board charged with executing strategic alliances which results in merging with several other organizations and becoming a subsidiary of merged organization; makes six-figure gift to organization
1999	Becomes vice chair of merged organization; resigns as board member of subsidiary
2004	Joins advisory board of subsidiary; continues as vice chair of merged organization
2008	Makes seven-figure capital campaign gift
2009	Becomes trustee emeritus subsidiary; retires as vice chair of merged organization
2010	Redrafts will to include planned gift to subsidiary
2011	To be determined

through to a period of postboard engagement. Tracing the career cycle of one of the board members studied over a period of years, this chart strikingly captures the idea that nonprofit engagement can be a lifelong affair of mutual fulfillment.

Questions the Trustee Should Ask

Nonprofit governance is very different from for-profit governance in many respects. Following are some broad questions the nonprofit trustee should ask (these will be elaborated on in the following chapters).

- In the absence of financial earnings and numbers, does the organization have adequate surrogate performance measures?

- Does the organization have transparency on cash flows? Forecasts? Is cash clearly king?
- Is the board functioning effectively? Has it overcome challenges of size and multiplicity of committees?
- Do the board members really understand the organization's mission, its current relevance, and oversee the effectiveness of its implementation?
- Are all members of the board giving adequately of their time, talent, and treasure?
- Is the relationship between the chair and CEO helping the organization achieve its mission?

2

MISSION

Nothing is more important for a new nonprofit board member to do than to take time to clearly understand the organization's mission and its complexity. Only then can the member begin to appropriately evaluate organization performance. For this reason, we have chosen to begin this book with a discussion of mission identification.

For the new nonprofit board member, the first step toward being effective is to deeply internalize the organization's mission (for both social impact–focused and member-focused organizations) and understand the thinking and passion behind it. Reading the written mission statement (we assume one exists) is the necessary first step but only the first step. The new board member needs to probe other board members as well as members of staff as to what they think the mission statement means in practice, eliciting as many specific examples as possible of what it has influenced. This is particularly important because in the absence of a P&L statement, which is standard in the for-profit world, it becomes the key fulcrum against which to measure performance. The board needs to understand what products and services are being delivered to key constituencies and whether these products or services are fulfilling the mission. At the core the mission statement provides the context for

- Evaluation of investment decisions
- Evaluation of proposals for expansion of some services

- Evaluation of potential curtailing or elimination of specific services
- Evaluation of the organization's cost-effectiveness for delivering services

These are critical perspectives for the new board member because often the core elements of the mission may create the largest financial challenges for the organization. Two examples: An all-girls high school knowingly rejected the overture to merge with an all-boys school and thus become coed. Although the proposal was overwhelmingly financially attractive, it would have meant abandoning a well-researched and deeply held belief by the board that there were special advantages to all-girls education. A new board member who had not participated in these discussions too quickly and glibly argued for the financially attractive choice of coeducation, thus simultaneously appearing out of touch and insensitive. The board member was ultimately ineffective, digging himself a hole he was never able to extract himself from. His first year would have been better spent trying to understand the perspectives of his fellow board members and administration. This would have involved a lot of listening, questioning, and reading. A well-informed naysayer is very useful. A naysayer, however, who has not done his or her homework is both an embarrassment and ineffective.

In a similar vein, a major world-class full-service hospital's first move after affiliating with another full-service world-class hospital was to add a large birthing center in an already saturated market, using scarce funds for the purpose (its new partner already had a birthing center). The hospital's purpose for building the birthing center was to be seen as a coequal provider with its partner in all areas and ensure that the coequal partners would not become differentiated by service type but would only cooperate in nonmedical ways, such as contract negotiations, endowment management, and so on. A decade later, they can be said to have been highly successful in this regard. Soundly rationalized in its full-service mission, it wanted to ensure that its reputation would not be compromised or abused by its partner. This view was not clear either to new board members, the community, or competitors at the time of investment. All now ruefully acknowledge the wisdom of what was done.

Performance against mission becomes a critical item for the board to focus on in its regular monitoring. In each situation, a combination of cash flow, service, and quality metrics must be put together to measure and assess performance. The absence of these metrics can lead to great misunderstandings concerning performance. These indicators will be discussed in more detail in Chapters Three and Four.

For the most part, there are not good missions or bad missions in aggregate. There are well-thought-out and internalized missions for some organizations. In other organizations, unfortunately, the mission statement has been hastily cobbled together with little thought. If well-crafted in an intense collaborative process and then communicated throughout the organization, the mission statement gives an organization identity, informs its capital investment decisions, and allows it to prioritize operating expenses. Performance on all these items as appropriate can be communicated to its staff, its clients, and financial supporters, as well as to local and state regulators, bond insurers, and so on.

As a board member, when talking about the organization's role and reason for being, you should be able to talk articulately about its mission, as well as provide examples of a half-dozen incidents where the mission has guided action. In so doing, you have to accept the messiness and inherent ambiguities in this process. Mission performance assessment is different from P&L but no less rigorous. In hospitals, for example, every month and quarter, the board sees inpatient and outpatient volumes against budget by service line. It sees intensity of case mix (and trends), quality performance statistics (and trends), cash flow against budget by line item, staff turnover, and philanthropy. In totality these metrics allow an informed assessment of progress. The following sections elaborate on critical challenges in defining performance against mission in much more detail.

Mission Is a Living Process

As noted in Chapter One, effective mission statements are much more than documents to be put on walls and on the front of annual reports. They are the product of intense debate among and between key constituencies as to who we are and what we value. Their preparation requires 360-degree discussions between board, staff, community, beneficiaries, and other interested bodies. Several factors can trigger a mission review which should be done at least every several years.

Organizational reaccreditation: The beginning of a reaccreditation process is a natural time to raise and discuss these issues and many accreditation groups expect this to be done before their team comes on site.

Appointment of a new CEO: A natural time to do a mission review is around the appointment of a new CEO. Sometimes it is done as part of a search committee's work to sharpen their thinking before they begin the process of selecting CEO candidates. Alternatively, after the new CEO arrives, his or her participation in a mission review process is often a good front end to a planning process that will enhance collaboration and help define the CEO's agenda for the next several years.

A good example of this is the case of an urban, land-starved, very academically elite school. When the new head was appointed, an issue that came to the fore was whether its almost one-hundred-year-old campus should be moved to a suburban setting to provide space for expansion of enrollment and more athletic facilities. As the debate went on and appropriate data were gathered, it became clear that the move would require tremendous financial resources that would detract from student financial aid and would create a transportation issue for gifted inner city students, making it harder for them to attend school. In short, the move would not improve anything that was at the heart of the school's mission. The idea was shelved. Instead, a $30 million capital campaign was launched and completed to improve financial aid and teachers' salaries. The decision to consider moving the school was deferred for at least another generation. The involvement of the board, the CEO, and, ultimately, outside facilitators was critical in getting the school to the point. Always the mission was at the center of the discussion.

Appointment of a new board chair: In a setting where the CEO has been there for a while, an activist board's nominating committee may choose a particular kind of chair to deliberately create friction and shake things up. This was recently done at a social services agency, ultimately leading to a new management team within two years.

The central point underlying each of these examples is that mission must be a vibrant living document that is periodically and meaningfully readdressed. This is because board members change, the external world changes, laws change, and so forth. Each of these changes requires going back and challenging or reaffirming an organization's mission and values. As a practical administrative matter, this is often done at the front end of an annual or biannual board or administrative retreat built around small-group discussions, followed by consideration by the whole group of a summary of the discussions. This process is usually facilitated either by trustees or trained outsiders. The richness of these discussions can be truly transforming. From one year to another, the format for such discussions must be changed to jar people out of their ruts into creative thinking and challenging their implicit (and often unrecognized) assumptions. Along the way, at all costs, a board must avoid the trap of falling into empty, boring, idealistic, interminable navel-gazing discussions.

Clarity of Mission Focus: A Powerful Action Enabler

Mission focus can lead to dramatically transforming decisions. A decade ago, the board of the California Academy of Science concluded that its mission of delivering world-class research and exhibits was being hurt by an aged facility that could not be effectively improved by small incremental actions. In an act of extraordinary leadership and vision, and taking a great risk, they decided to move all facilities (including a large aquarium) to a temporary location ten miles away and one quarter the size of the original location, and to demolish and completely replace the old facility. They operated at a much diminished level over four years in the temporary facility while they raised over $300 million in philanthropy and constructed a new state-of-the-art facility (a size they had never envisioned before) to complement its twenty-first-century mission. The project is now completed and the organization thrives in its new facility.

Similarly, a major secondary school recently appointed a board committee to review its science program. Over six months of collection and analysis of a lot of data, the committee concluded the existing program was not in the world-class traditions of the school. This triggered a total redesign of the program during a time of financial stress and resulted in a campaign to raise $27 million for new physical facilities in the face of many other priorities. Mission recommitment and alignment of investment to it was at the heart of this decision. Sadly, these are hard, complex decisions difficult to incorporate into a net present value analysis.

Mission Achievement

Achieving one's mission completely is not an unmitigated blessing and can, ironically, pose terrible challenges. For example, in the 1950s, the March of Dimes' entire mission was focused on finding a cure for an enormous scourge of that time, polio. Dramatically successful in achieving this mission, it funded the breakthrough research of Doctors Salk and Sabin. A cure for polio was found and the March of Dimes was left with a powerful fund-raising machine and no mission. Although shutting it down was an obvious solution, instead it morphed into funding research to understand and prevent birth defects. The March of Dimes, for a period, was a fund-raising organization in search of a mission.

Mission Impracticality

Wheaton College in Norton, Massachusetts, had been a women's college since its inception. Despite a strong faculty and a recently completed capital campaign, it faced significant reduction in both number and quality of students. The board ultimately decided its future as a women's college was not viable and voted to make it coeducational. Despite angst among the student body and some of the alumnae, today it is thriving with a strong student body, a vibrant curriculum, and a balanced budget. Almost all now agree that the right decision was made years earlier. Changing tastes and interests of prospective applicants had simply overtaken the viability of the women's education part of the mission for this college in a remote rural town. Although often clear afterward, at the time these decisions can be bitter and emotional.

Mission Vision

Particularly critical is the ability to look ahead and see the emergence of social forces that will make today's mission impractical or worse. The fact that everything seems fine on the surface today does not mean that all is well. The case study about Mt. Auburn Hospital is illustrative of the defensive actions that can be taken when an organization looks far into the future.

Mt. Auburn Hospital

In 1993, the two largest hospitals in Boston—Massachusetts General Hospital and Brigham and Women's Hospital—merged, creating an entity called Partners with potentially huge negotiating power over health insurers.

The impact on its competitors in the region was dramatic. Take, for example, the Mt. Auburn Hospital. In 1995 the Mt. Auburn Hospital, 125 years old, was a mid-tier 270-bed hospital in Cambridge, Massachusetts, with a combination of community hospital and partial tertiary care capabilities. It had had fourteen years of steady positive cash flow from operations and possessed a reasonably strong balance sheet. Nonetheless, the board was alarmed by this powerful new competitor and launched a full-scale consultant-supported review of their likely market position and operating efficiencies over the next decade. Substantial effort was devoted to analyzing other hospital markets in the country for signs of leading-edge trends that could affect them. The results of the study were disturbing. Every trend across the country suggested Mt. Auburn had insufficient critical mass to survive in the complicated and rapidly consolidating hospital market of eastern Massachusetts. After intense debate during numerous meetings, the board, with the unanimous concurrence of physicians and administrators, concluded that the hospital was overly exposed in this new world and needed partners to give them critical mass to negotiate better contracts with health insurers. A year later, they merged with a much larger hospital group that had a strong balance sheet and critical mass for negotiations with insurers. Two years after the merger, the cost trends forecast by the initial study had a dramatic impact on Mt. Auburn, leading to an $11 million loss followed by significant additional losses the next year. In the light of these subsequent developments, had the merger not taken place, the hospital could well have closed as it incurred devastating costs which would have prevented it from meeting its loan obligations. As part of a larger organization, Mt. Auburn had time to restructure and redeploy, and today it is a stable, vibrant organization. Their five closest geographic competitors active in 1995 are all gone. Four went bankrupt and the fifth survived with the aid of public support. In this case, by surrendering the part of the mission associated with independence, they were able to continue providing vital medical services to the community. In 2010, however, Partners still casts a shadow over the competitive scene through its ability to extract special price concessions from insurers.

Organizations Can Become Excessively Focused Inward (Mission Drift)

Without a jolt, an organization can either drift down a trajectory of simply not challenging the validity of existing processes that are no longer appropriate, or slowly drift off mission year by year. An excellent example is an old-time educational establishment. A new CEO came to the organization that had been in operation over one hundred years. At a very demanding educational day and boarding school, the number of day students had grown while boarders had stagnated in both number and quality over the previous two decades. The board was vaguely aware of this but had not focused closely on the change as it had happened so slowly, and hadn't really registered in their minds as an actionable issue. The new CEO immediately focused on and grasped this as an issue and launched a series of meetings which ultimately led to a two-day off-site meeting to focus on this challenge and brainstorm alternate solutions. The solutions were stark. Either eliminate boarding and become only a day school or, alternatively, invest heavily in new dorms, dining facilities, and programmatic activities to make the campus an active vibrant place on weekends as well as weekdays and provide buzz to the boarding program. This second approach would require raising financial resources on a scale they had never tried before. After intense discussion leading up and through the two-day meeting, it was reaffirmed that boarding was a vital part of the school's mission. Furthermore, research suggested that with the right dormitory facilities in place, the school could recruit students in sufficient numbers and of appropriate abilities. Finally, with the aid of substantial professional consulting, they concluded it would be possible to raise the necessary money over a period of years. The decision to proceed was made. This led to major fund-raising, building of new dormitories, and expansion of admission and recruiting activities. Eight years later, the investment can be said to be an unqualified success with all goals achieved. It also caused intense pain in one constituency because there were now fewer spots for local day children, leading to anxiety among local parents. Had the implications of the mission not been fully grasped by the board, the decision to revitalize the boarding school would not have taken place, and the situation would have deteriorated irretrievably.

Embedded Dry Rot Can Creep in (Mission Drift)

A school with great success in college admissions had built its reputation around its strength in the humanities. Based on a mission statement focusing on excellence in all elements of a liberal arts education, the school head became concerned that the science program seemed mired in educational concepts of twenty years earlier. This led to the appointment of a trustee-led ad hoc committee, composed of trustees, several outside experts, and science faculty. Over fifteen meetings, large amounts of data were collected. This included comparisons with other schools, surveys of outside research literature, and surveys of all alumni of the past ten years concerning their views of the educational experience (alumni turned out to be heavily dissatisfied with their training in this area). The committee recommended a complete reconfiguration of the science program, which took four years to execute as a new curriculum had to be installed one year at a time beginning with the ninth grade. Heavy but less mission-strategic investments were deferred in other areas in order to bring this important part of mission execution up to speed. It is not as much fun to invest in this kind of catch-up mode on mission execution as it is to plow new ground, but it may be absolutely vital.

Mission Can Become Diffuse

Mission review can identify distracting or peripheral activities that are diverting attention from the core. However, absent a financial crisis, it may be very hard to deal with these activities, as they often have their own very vocal constituencies who argue passionately, but not always accurately, that these activities are at the core of the organization's mission, regardless of financial constraints. Defusing such arguments can be very painful and consume inordinate energy. Not infrequently these activities were created as a result of opportunistically accepting restricted gifts from funding sources. The funding source then disappears and the organization is left with a series of incoherent activities. A head of a social services agency ruefully noted to the authors that her current portfolio of activities was completely shaped by funding opportunities, rather than by rigorous discipline on understanding community needs first and then pushing for appropriately targeted funding. Regrettably money is often accepted when it should not have been.

Refocusing on mission is very painful when embedded conflicting constituencies exist. In a real sense, in these situations hemorrhaging cash can be a significant advantage if you are trying to force change; cash loss signifies that a crisis is at hand. Otherwise you may wind up simply frozen in the status quo. The absence of a crisis may mean that no matter how worthwhile, a change cannot be thoughtfully examined.

Mission Viability Can Erode

Circumstances external or internal to the organization may conspire to make a previously viable mission no longer viable. A painful case in point was the simultaneous merger of three hospitals done with the explicit mission of providing an integrated health care system that would provide high-quality, cost-effective health services to the community. It was envisioned that there would be a common integrated health and medical infrastructure across the three previously independent hospitals. This would mean that, among other things, there would be common medical unit heads in the system, common administrative and medical protocols, and a common negotiating posture with all health insurers. The mission was clear and seemed unassailable to many, as it had been done in other settings. The fatal mistake was that the CEO of one of the hospitals was put in charge and, without exception, all key medical and administrative appointments came from his hospital although in many respects the other two had better administrative and medical protocols. The political pain was so intense, and the impact on finances so difficult that, two CEOs later, the merged hospital had become simply a hospital holding company with a small central staff and all key staffing and medical decisions still being made in the three local hospitals. The holding company became responsible for residual activities like IT, audit, managing the combined endowment, and the managing and refinancing of the debt. The original mission was lost in the ugliness of the attempted merger activities. Viable today, however, its trustees remain concerned but have also largely abandoned any hope of executing the original vision for at least another decade. An unhappy taste of reality.

Mission No Longer Aligns with Reality

A midsize hospital prized its association with a leading medical school and broadly advertised the connection, which was very important to a number of its patients and financial supporters. The operational reality, however, was very different. Only three faculty had appointments at the hospital. One was a seventy-two-year-old psychiatrist winding down his career and the other two were instructors who had almost no publication records. When the time came to select a new chief of medicine, a vast majority of the doctors in the hospital wanted to hire one of the instructors who was a superb teacher, but almost without publications. The board, however, recognized that the medical school relationship was a critical part of the mission and that the medical school at that time was overwhelmingly oriented towards research professors rather than teaching professors. Continuing on their current trajectory could potentially have cost the hospital its interns and its medical school link. Armed with this perspective, the board pushed back very hard on the local candidate and insisted on a national search, which ultimately brought a world-class scholar to the hospital. It is impossible to overstate the pain and disruption this caused, leading to intense turmoil in the medical staff and a virtual vote of no confidence in the board by the medical staff, as a result of their affection for their old colleague and their dislike for the new director. Within weeks of his appointment, the new head had established his credibility and the argument was forgotten. Today, four more full professors now work in the hospital and the links with the medical school have been completely reestablished. Interestingly, the medical school has now come to recognize the importance of teaching, and the "old instructor" now holds a chair as a "distinguished educator." As an outside board member, a key role is to make sure that local wisdom does not lead to long-term destruction of capabilities. Without really knowing it, an organization can become disconnected from reality through either ignorance or neglect.

Mission Becomes Undoable Due to Changing External Environment

The most thoughtful and worthy of missions can be eviscerated by changing external factors, be they cultural, legal, or environmental. An excellent example of this is the case history of two urban adoption agencies. By the mid-1960s, the agencies had had decades of experience in placing babies in families who for the most part could not have children. The combination of the development of the birth control pill and the changing attitudes of single mothers toward deciding to keep their babies drastically reduced the flow of American babies for adoption, leading first to the merger of the two organizations and then a sharp refocusing of the mission of the surviving one away from adoption toward social services. Board members need to be especially sensitive to these issues in a changing world as sometimes the people who remain on the front lines for ideological reasons may be in a state of denial regarding what is really going on.

Ability to Achieve Mission Is Eroded by Too Rapid Growth

In these cases, the mission is appropriate but the cause is so compelling that the organization exceeds its capacity by trying to expand too rapidly and thus loses control over quality. This is the core challenge embedded in a recently completed study of the Clontarf Foundation in Australia.[1] A major societal problem in Australia is the very high rate of school drop-outs among aboriginal boys, and their consequent inability to gain employment, which leads to drug and alcohol dependency and crimes committed to support both habits. The insight of Clontarf (led by a former professional Australian football player and coach) was that boys would stay in school if this allowed them to participate in competitive organized football. You could only practice and play football if you regularly went to class. The early schools set up by the foundation were dramatically effective in keeping the boys in school and in opening up a wide variety of post-graduate employment opportunities. It really worked! The foundation is now actively raising money to scale up the initial school successes into franchises to be located across Australia. Their dominant challenge beyond raising money is how to run the greatly expanded number of schools in a way where quality is maintained and monitored. This is a happy but real challenge.

Mission Broadened Too Much

Sometimes far-off projects can get in the way of local needs. A church facing this problem is located in an affluent suburb of a city which has desperate problems in its inner city including poverty, child neglect, and access to quality education. The church in its wisdom has chosen a significant focus on boys in a South American country who are being brought up in desperate circumstances. The church has funded a wonderful school for these boys in grades K through 8. It is a heartwarming project where teams of parishioners make one-week trips to South America to help with education and building facilities. They are now trying to raise additional money from church members to be able to do more. The question to be addressed in this process is how much of the resources should be allocated to church maintenance and facilities, how much to meet local needs for community programs, and how much to worthwhile foreign activities. Sorting the mission intent out here is hard because some people will only focus their energy on the geographically remote and exotic activity. The result is that a complex portfolio of expenditures may emerge that seems incoherent to the observer but actually has a lot of logic. How to encourage mission coherence without losing volunteer support and funds is a real challenge; there are no universal or easy answers. This discussion of these issues is especially complex for the new board member because it is both nuanced and embedded in history, of which she is largely unaware.

Mission Expansion Is Unmanaged

Sometimes, when you hope to expand the mission, you look for demonstration projects that can mobilize resources, donors, and delivery of an inspiring project which will motivate other donors for other projects. A good example of this is the Barbara Harris Camp and Conference Center of the Episcopal Diocese of Eastern Massachusetts. A new bishop was seeking to dramatically expand the diocesan activities into areas that local parishes were not capable of supporting. He conceived of an $18 million project to bring a summer camp religious experience to the children in the parishes as well as provide a year-round conference facility for retreats, vestry meetings, and so forth. The project was viable by itself and consistent with diocesan mission. By undertaking this effort, however, the diocese hoped that the dramatic impact and visibility of the camp and conference center would attract funding for other projects also related to mission—projects that, though lacking the same intuitive appeal, might have even more of an impact from a mission perspective. The camp and conference center was enormously successful. The money was raised, the facility built, and after three years all its programs are full. Equally important, it showed in a tangible way to the nearly two hundred churches in the diocese and their parishioners the value of a diocesan initiative in accomplishing something no one church could do by itself. Other worthwhile projects have followed at the diocesan level including urban ministries and campus outreach programs to attract young adults. In this case, the first project was not necessarily the one closest to mission fulfillment, but its success was necessary to create the climate to generate the money and support for these subsequent and perhaps even more mission-relevant projects. Executing mission sometimes involves a chess game of moves that interrelate in very complex ways.

Mission Conflict

A delicate minuet of irreconcilable conflict of missions can arise between organizations with overlapping constituencies. In the Episcopal Church, for example, the National Church, the Diocese of Eastern Massachusetts, and several churches within the

Diocese of Eastern Massachusetts are all having simultaneous annual campaigns and capital campaigns. In reality all three organizations are going after the same donor base. Each to some extent wishes the other two were not in the fund-raising business because it believes they are hurting its efforts and ability to fulfill mission. The reality is that with three organizations asking, the total amount of money raised is turning out to be greater than could be done without multiple initiatives. In part this is because at any point one of the three organizations may be out of favor, for a variety of reasons, with any individual donor. Another reason is that some people are driven and inspired more by a "local" mission whereas others are inspired by a "national" or even "international" view. The reality is a complex, ambiguous, situation incapable of total transparency, where it is argued that the three organizations collectively do more good than would be accomplished if only the churches were doing the fund-raising.

Mission Not in Public Interest

Sometimes an organization's mission and efforts to fulfill it may create situations where the public interest is not fully fulfilled. Partners Healthcare, the largest health system in Massachusetts, is a case in point. Its mission is to be "committed to serving the community. We are dedicated to enhancing patient care, teaching and research and to taking a leadership role in an integrated health care system. We recognize that increasing value and improving quality are essential to maintaining quality." What could be wrong with this? Plenty, as it turns out. Formed in 1995 as the merger of the two premier hospitals in a seven-hospital market, they were able to bring special pricing pressures on the health insurers and extract concessions far beyond what other hospitals could do, a fact which has lasted to 2010 and is a current matter of great publicity and controversy. In fact, when one health insurer tried to drop Partners as a high-cost hospital because of their costs, employers forced them to back off because it was so disruptive to their employees. That is the good news. The bad news is the eight-hundred-pound gorilla put unbearable pressure on the other five surviving competitor hospitals that resulted in their receiving sharply lower reimbursement from the insurers. In the cold light of a decade's history, a strong argument can be made that the Massachusetts regulator should have stepped in, prevented the merger in 1995, and instead encouraged the two partners MGH and Brigham and Women's Hospital to each become the center of its own network, facilitating the emergence of a market of two to three competitors of roughly equal size, as has happened in other hospital markets in the United States. What was best for the two hospitals may ultimately have caused real problems for the community and, ultimately, the consumers.

Summary

In short, mission identification is at the heart of the nonprofit board's work. These paragraphs highlight the importance of mission for a nonprofit on the one hand and its great complexity in being defined and executed on the other hand. Understanding these nuances is at the heart of a new trustee's becoming an effective member and eventually a leader on the board. An uninformed fixation only on short-term cash flows can lead to poor results for the organization in terms of its viability. Chapters Three and Four will focus on the issues of measuring performance against mission.

Questions the Trustee Should Ask

Deep, internalized understanding of mission is key to being an effective trustee. Key questions the trustee must ask include:

- Has the mission been recently reexamined? The world changes.

- Is the organization on mission or has it drifted off target over time?
- Has the organization become sluggish in its pursuit of mission?
- Has the organization added too many peripheral activities not focused on mission?
- Are the aspirations of the mission still viable? Is the mission unachievable in the changing world?
- Is the organization losing its mission focus by growing too rapidly?
- Conversely, has the organization expanded its mission scope appropriately as it grows?
- Are differing aspects of the organization's mission in conflict with each other?
- Is the organization's mission and its execution aligned with public interest?
- Are the organization's performance measures aligned with public interest?

3

PERFORMANCE MEASUREMENT

You have just completed six months on the board and have attended three board meetings. You've unraveled just enough of the mysteries of fund accounting to begin to feel comfortable about the finances of the organization (from time to time the business manager still pulls an accounting rabbit out of the hat). You are comfortable that the coming year's budget has been carefully and responsibly put together and that there is clear buy-in for the strategic plan for the next three years. You have made what is for you a significant financial pledge to the organization. Your fellow board members for the most part have turned out to be very stimulating. The board and committee meetings, although often a bit meandering, have remained on target and are providing both adequate input and oversight to the organization.

With all that said, however, two questions bother you. Are we really delivering on our mission, not just meeting budget, and are we getting maximum impact from our expenditures? These are deeply important questions that lie at the very heart of nonprofit governance. They are so important, in fact, that we choose deliberately to address them before finance (covered in Chapter Four). Performance measurement is an area where current practice has been very spotty and uneven, and a number of organizations have not even tried to address it. Indeed, for many organizations the reality is that the contents of this chapter are aspirational with current reality far behind what we are advocating. We believe this is both irresponsible and a mistake. This area is one where we believe that the trustees can provide powerful impetus to get started and represents one of the most important areas for improvement in 2011.

This chapter gives you a methodology to determine whether what your organization is doing is appropriate; alternatively, it can serve as a tool kit to get started. We will introduce our approach around a nonprofit which is focused on providing safe places and other services to abused women with children. Somewhat more briefly, we will apply it to two other settings illustrating the performance metrics they use that go beyond budget performance. We hope that the composite of these lists of performance measures will lead you to get started on an appropriate initiative in your organization, if it does not currently have appropriate performance metrics for the board's use.

Resource Acquisition and Impact

To start the development of performance metrics we begin by grouping the organization's resource gathering and disbursing activities into five clusters. (For more extensive discussion on nonprofit performance measures, see Epstein and Rejc Buhovac[1] from which much of this chapter is drawn.) The key components of these clusters are shown in Figure 3.1.

Inputs

Inputs are all the key tangible and intangible things that are brought into the nonprofit to enable it to perform its tasks. They include cash, personnel, equipment, and other material items. It also includes the mission statement (if you don't have one, you need one) and strategy (if you don't have an articulated one,

Figure 3.1 Resource Acquisition and Impact Chart

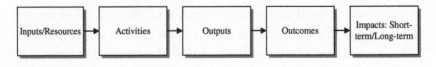

you need one). It includes a keen understanding of who are the other providers of service similar to yours and how you stack up against them. Finally, it includes the current depth and breadth of your board's and staff's understanding of these items. Often, as will be discussed, there are serious misalignment of views between various members of the board and staff which, until addressed through discussions, can seriously impede the development of progress.

Activities

Activities are all the specific programs and tasks that the organization undertakes. Considerable art is required to group these programs and tasks into meaningful clusters for analysis. Indeed, as the world changes over time, the clusters may have to be reconstructed in different ways to facilitate new analyses for the altered situation. For example, a school at one time broke itself into segments respectively titled "off-campus programs"—music school, riding program, and core academic activities. This facilitated the board's asking hard questions about the viability of each of these key activities and led to significant trimming and investment. At a later time, the school was facing a world of intense academic competition and tight financial resources. After considerable debate, the board and staff divided the core academic activities into groupings that included classroom services, technology, library services, residential services, athletic programs, development activities, and more. These groupings helped trigger intense debate about the appropriate balance between these activities and led to a number of adjustments between board and staff.

Outputs

Outputs are the tangible and intangible products and services delivered as a result of the organization's activities. For a school, it might be number of graduates, type and quality of college placements, success of alumni in college, number of major disciplinary situations, number of applications to the school, success in recruiting faculty and staff, and school morale. The selection of these specific outputs for any institution would vary by its mission, core competencies, and strategy inputs. When the world changes, as discussed in the previous paragraph, these measured outputs may no longer be exactly the right ones to focus on, and may need to be modified.

Outcomes

Outcomes are the specific change in behaviors and individuals affected by the delivery of these services and products. Again, for a secondary school, outcomes would be such items as alumni outperforming in college beyond what would be indicated by their initial test scores and achievements, an increase in applications reflecting parent and student enthusiasm for the product, a surge in financial support linked to recognition of school's programs, or local and national awards on program excellence, and so on.

Impact

Are there benefits to communities and society as a whole as a result of these outcomes? For example, are parts of our programs now being emulated by other schools? Do our alumni take on important community leadership roles? Are textbooks and other teaching materials prepared by our faculty being used at other institutions, thus broadening our impact? Are numbers of our faculty and administrators asked to speak at industry meetings and the like? Are we doing well in appropriate industry benchmarking surveys?

Breaking the organization out into these pieces, though not earth-shattering, allows the development of a number of performance metrics which in aggregate give insight on how the organization is performing against mission.

The following paragraphs take this analysis and apply it to an organization that "provides safe places and services to abused women with children." The first step in its application was a series of brainstorming sessions first with staff only, then with the board alone, and finally with the two groups together under the leadership of a trained facilitator. The purpose of these sessions was to develop the imposing "Causal Linkage Map" shown in Figure 3.2. This map teased out the key components of the Resource Acquisition and Impact Chart. Each item on the map is discussed in the following paragraphs.

Figure 3.2 The Mission Effectiveness Approach: The Causal Linkage Map of Impact Drivers for Providing Safe Places and Services to Abused Women with Children

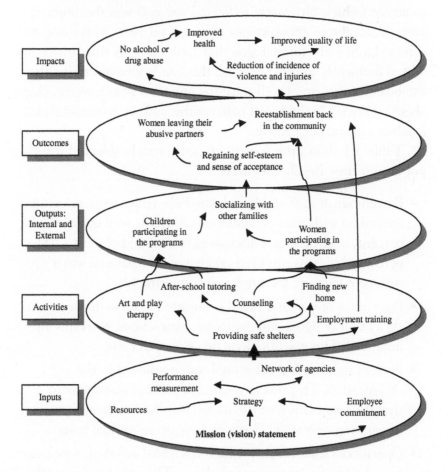

A very difficult section to prepare was Inputs; impassioned debates took place about the key elements of mission and strategy. In this case, there was a network of a dozen other agencies in the city trying to do roughly the same thing. This led to intense discussions as to what was our niche and was it viable? Intense battles took place between staff and board. What the staff wanted to do, the board did not feel was economically viable. What the board wanted to do, the staff did not feel was on mission. The good news was there was a facilitator and a process which brought these sentiments to the surface and allowed them to be sorted out. In other settings which have been discussed in the book, this was not possible and led to unfortunate results. The key performance indicator (which ultimately indicated success) was the improvement in employee commitment over several years in the annual survey. Unlike all the dialogue that took place in this situation, all too frequently in other settings the staff begins muttering that the board is a group of well-meaning amateurs who have no clue about reality while the board believes the staff are narrow-minded localists with no perspective.

Table 3.1 shows the four metrics ultimately selected for input monitoring. Briefly they were

- Percentage of staff and board who believe strategic priorities are linked with mission statement. Initially well under 50 percent, over time and discussion this moved closer to 100 percent. This was surveyed on an annual basis and was a surrogate measure for employee commitment.
- Percentage of staff and board committed to mission execution. As a result of significant discussion over several years this also improved. This was also done on an annual basis.
- Percentage of new professional staff employed in the organization. This was to remind board and management that the faster this rose the more effort had to be put into integrating new staff. This was done on an annual basis.
- Operational sustainability, which was added as a simple measure to make sure finances were in balance. This was done quarterly.

Table 3.1 The Mission Effectiveness Approach: Examples of Performance Measures for Providing Safe Places and Other Services to Abused Women with Children

Categories	Performance Measures
Inputs	Number (%) of strategic priorities aligned with the mission statement Number (%) of employees committed to achieving the mission Increase in staff employed company-wide (%) Operational sustainability (operating revenue as a percentage of costs)
Activities	Dollars spent on providing safe places to stay Dollars spent on women-related activities Dollars spent on children-related activities Dollars spent on family-related activities Employee productivity
Outputs	Number (%) of women participating in the programs offered Number (%) of children participating in the programs offered Number (%) of families socializing with other families like them
Outcomes	Number (%) of women leaving their abusive partners Number (%) of women successfully entering new jobs Number (%) of abused families setting up a new home Number (%) of children reestablishing themselves in their communities
Impacts	Number (%) of beneficiaries reporting the reduction of incidence of violence Number (%) of beneficiaries reporting the reduction of impact of injuries and violence Number (%) of beneficiaries safe from alcohol abuse Number (%) of beneficiaries safe from underage drinking Number (%) of beneficiaries safe from abuse and illicit use of drugs Number (%) of beneficiaries reporting major improvement in quality of life

The section on Activities started with a broad-based identification of what were ultimately determined to be the six main activities that the organization offered. These were to provide safe shelters, art and play therapy, after-school tutoring, counseling, finding new homes, and employment training. In this case, these happened to correspond with the six organization units but this was not necessary; rather, with much more art than science in the process, board and staff determined collectively that these were the six principal activities the board needed to monitor to ensure that the organization was going in the right direction. These six activities were then clustered into three groups relating to family, children, and women. Every quarter the board looked at the trends in these numbers with the objective of identifying and evaluating any significant variations and what this meant for the organization's performance as a whole. A final measure was on employee productivity, calculated as cases per employee. Trends in either direction were a matter of discussion. For example, more cases per employee might mean that in aggregate, individual cases were not getting enough attention, whereas fewer cases per employee could be a signal on overstaffing.

Outputs were captured monthly in three categories. The first was the number of children in these families who participated in the after-school training or art and play therapy, or both. The second was the number of families (self-reported) who socialized with one or more families per week. The third was the number of women who participated either in counseling or employment training each month. Table 3.1 identifies the percentage metrics on these items that were reported each month. The hope was that over time these metrics would either stay stable or trend upwards.

Outcomes were measured by the success of the program participants' taking tangible progress toward improvement in their lives. This included obtaining new jobs, setting up a new home, and reestablishing themselves in their communities.

Impacts were broadly defined as reduction in alcohol or drug abuse, improved health, improved quality of life, and reduction of incidents of violence and injuries for the population as a whole. As surrogate measures for these items each quarter, the actual women being served were questioned as to how they were being affected in these areas. Downward trends in these numbers were seen as signs of positive progress. Obviously this is an imperfect measure, but it was the best they could come up with for this situation.

In aggregate, these items make up the dashboard items that are monitored by staff and the board on a monthly, quarterly, and annual basis.

For illustrative purposes regarding how this approach has been applied in other settings, an additional two sets of causal maps and their associated performance measures are shown. The first, shown in Figure 3.3 and Table 3.2, are the maps and measures for a large

Figure 3.3 The Mission Effectiveness Model: The Causal Linkage Map of Impact Drivers for a Professional Association

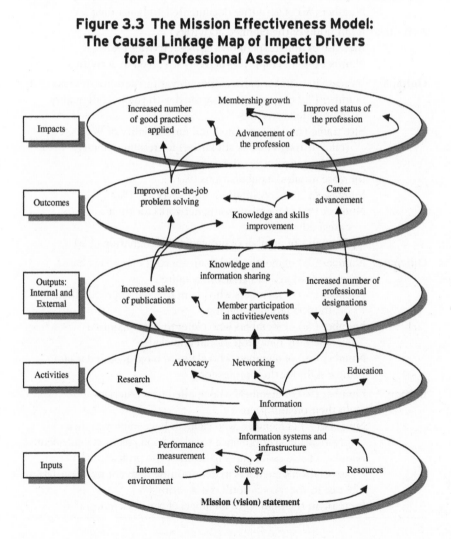

Table 3.2 The Mission Effectiveness Approach: Examples of Performance Measures for a Professional Association

Categories	Performance Measures
Inputs	Number (%) of strategic priorities aligned with the mission (vision)
	Growth in the number of full-time employees (%)
	Employee commitment to achieving the mission (vision)
	Operational sustainability (operating revenue as a percentage of costs)
	Dollars available for IT infrastructure investments
	Number (%) of activities documented and measured
Activities	Realization of the planned activities (%)
	Increase in dollars spent on various activities (%)
	Number (%) of employees actively involved in activities
Outputs	Increase in member participation in various activities/events (%)
	Number (%) of participants satisfied with the overall quality of provided activities
	Site traffic (number of visits) and functionality of Web site (click-through rate or stickiness) for resource library, member directories, and so forth
	Increase in sales of publications (%)
	Increase in staff consultations and advocacy (%)
	Number (%) of members using networks for their career advancement
	Increase in the number of professional designations (%)
Outcomes	Number (%) of members who advanced their careers based on professional designations acquired
	Number (%) of members who claim to have improved their on-the-job problem solving
	Number (%) of members who claim to have acquired significantly new professional knowledge
	Number (%) of members who claim to have acquired useful new skills for their profession
Impacts	Number (%) of members who applied new practices in their organizations
	Number (%) of members who claim to have improved their organization's performance based on good practices implemented
	Number of successful participations of the professional association's members in determining relevant new legislation
	Change in the association's status rating (%)
	Increase in the number of members of the association (%)

Figure 3.4 The Mission Effectiveness Model: The Causal Linkage Map of Impact Drivers for a University

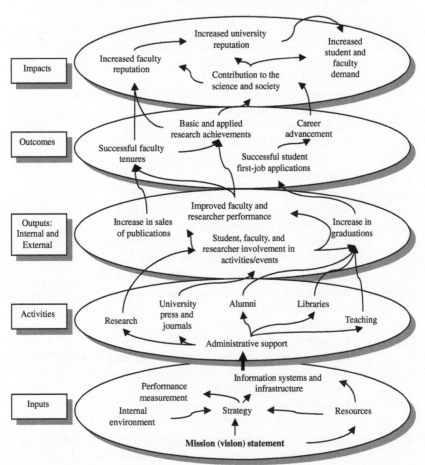

national professional association (a member-focused organization). The second, shown in Figure 3.4 and Table 3.3, are the maps and measures for a large research-oriented university (a social impact–focused organization). Very similar processes to those used in the organization for abused women were applied to develop this measure for these settings. In both cases the boards felt these measures to be useful in helping them to keep their fingers on the pulse of how mission fulfillment was being executed.

Table 3.3 The Mission Effectiveness Model: Examples of Performance Measures for a University

Categories	Performance Measures
Inputs	Number (%) of strategic priorities aligned with the mission (vision)
	Growth in the number of administrative support (%)
	Growth in endowments (%)
	Dollars available for IT infrastructure, hardware, and software investments
	Dollars available for research and teaching
	Number (%) of faculty and administration compensated based on individual or group performance
	Employee commitment
Activities	Realization of planned programs/courses (%)
	Realization of planned research projects (%)
	Realization of planned publications (%)
	Realization of planned investments in library resources (%)
	Hours of Web site down time (in a year)
	Increase in dollars spent on various activities (%)
Outputs	Increase in student involvement in various programs, courses, and events (%)
	Increase in student satisfaction (%)
	Increase in student graduation (%)
	Increase in researcher involvement in research projects (%)
	Increase in on-time completed research projects (%)
	Increase in sales of university press (%)
	Increase in sales of online articles (%)
	Click-through rate (stickiness) for online resources
Outcomes	Number (%) of students who successfully applied for their first job
	Number (%) of students who advanced their careers based on acquired graduation, completed management programs, etc.
	Number (%) of faculty with successful tenure
	Number (%) researchers who were granted research awards for their research contributions
Impacts	Number (%) of successful participations of the faculty and researchers in designing new legislation, rules, frameworks, and so forth
	Number (%) of faculty with distinguished reputation (based on endowments and other grants received)
	Change in the university's status rating (%)
	Increase in the number of high quality student applications (%)
	Increase the number and quality of faculty applications (%)

What these exhibits show in total is how organizations can and do build the bridge between the qualitative words of mission definition and the development of solid metrics that demonstrate how progress is being made on achieving mission. The detailed measures identified here are worth careful study on your part as you begin to think about appropriate measures for your organization. The arrows and the flow shown in the causal linkage maps are also important as they cause board members to carefully think through what actions they can take to achieve mission effectiveness. The following points are the major ones you should take away.

1. There is a clear proven methodology on how to go about establishing performance metrics. This methodology involves a lot of process and meetings, where both the board and staff work independently to generate the causal maps and then come up with a reconciled version. The process of reconciliation is critical and the end product by definition is somewhat subjective. A different group of board members and staff could come to somewhat different maps. This judgment and imprecision notwithstanding, the end result is much more useful than if nothing were attempted. In addition, the process of discussing each of these elements always produces new and important insights. As you look at the measures on the one hand, you can gain a lot of insight. On the other hand, you may also be slightly anxious about what you are not measuring that could be relevant.

2. These performance measures draw on a combination of financial numbers, activity rates (such as number of people in training sessions), and general indices provided by local, state, and national government agencies. There is not a science to identifying which clusters of activities are most meaningful to measure. Rather, items are clustered together in ways which the board after significant discussion comes to believe is useful. Over time as the environment and the

nonprofit change, previously meaningful groupings may become less useful and new ones have to be created.

3. Depending on the performance metric, some may be reported in time spans as short as a month and others as long as a year. In general, management needs more frequent and detailed performance metrics than the board does.

4. Comparative indices and activity levels comparing one nonprofit to other similar organizations are particularly useful but often very hard to gather. Hospitals and schools are examples of industries where a lot of comparative data is available and should be used. Use of this data may be slightly complicated because a low-performing organization may fudge a little in their reporting to delay word getting out about their problems. In some cases such as scholarship grants, there are clear laws about what can and cannot be shared between organizations so as to encourage competition for the best students.

In aggregate these three examples of applying mission effectiveness models, causal linkage maps, and performance measures illustrate the critical connection between a defined mission and strategy and the selection of which appropriate performance measures to execute. This approach is equally useful in both social impact–focused nonprofits and member-focused nonprofit organizations. Examples of both kinds of nonprofit organizations were included in Chapter One in the discussions of KaBOOM! and CMA Canada. Two additional examples with demonstrated best practices (Opportunity International and AARP) are discussed below.

Opportunity International is a large and growing microfinance network with the mission "To provide opportunities for people in chronic poverty to transform their lives."[2] This is a social mission, but financial sustainability is critical to its achievement. The network's success is based on financial

sustainability, donor funding, good microfinance partners, training, tapping business leaders, gaining massive scale and rapid
growth, and empowering people locally. It uses various performance metrics to measure success and guide strategy in pursuit of
its financial excellence. These performance measures are complemented by a set of nonfinancial performance measures which
attempt to capture the organization's success in improving its
clients' economic, social, and spiritual life (see Table 3.4). The
Opportunity International performance measurement system
contains

- Indicators of economic performance, that refer to the impact
  that micro-lending has on clients
- Indicators of social performance that help understand
  whether the poor are better off in more fundamental ways
  after they became clients
- Indicators of spiritual dimension, which is at the core of the
  organization's mission

AARP (formerly the American Association of Retired Per-
sons) is the largest nonprofit membership organization for people age fifty and over in the United States with the mission of
"enhancing the quality of life for all as we age." Activities are
carried out by AARP and the AARP Foundation, which
administers various charitable programs and legal services for
older Americans, including those who are not members of
AARP.[3]

The AARP Foundation measures its performance using four
perspectives: (1) "Resources and Stewardship," to reflect the
Foundation's status and associated standards; (2) "People" perspective, (3) "Social Impact and Value," capturing the organization's focus on promoting social change and adding value to the
lives of older Americans; and (4) "Organizational Leadership
and Integration," highlighting the Foundation's focus on

Table 3.4 Opportunity International Performance Measures[4]

Perspective	Performance Measures
Financial perspective	Operational sustainability (operating revenue as a percentage of costs)* Number of loan clients at year-end Dollars loaned per year Average loan size/Average first loan size Number (%) of loans made to women Dollars spent on client training and education Client retention (%) Financial sustainability (ability to cover lending expenses and the cost of capital) Portfolio quality: Number (%) of arrears over 30 days Return on equity or incremental benefit to society Loan repayment rate, and so on
Client economic perspective	Number (%) of new clients or businesses per year Increase in sales Increase in profits (%) Amount of voluntary savings Number of jobs created per year
Client social perspective	Number (%) of clients with increased civic/leadership involvement Training/Education: Number (%) of clients with successful completion of training/education Number (%) of clients with better nutrition Number (%) of clients with improved housing Number (%) of clients aware of HIV/AIDS Empowerment rate**
Client spiritual perspective	Number (%) of clients claiming they improved their relationship with God, based on successful economic and social life Improvement in quality of life (%) Increase in worship participation (%)

*Operational sustainability does not take into account the cost to borrow the money that an organization lends at market interest rate. Financial sustainability, on the other hand, includes lending expenses and the cost of capital.

**Empowerment can be defined as the involvement of employees in the decision-making process as measured by questionnaires.

Table 3.5 The AARP Foundation Performance Indicator[5]

Perspectives	Performance Measures
Resources and stewardship	Amount ($) raised for charitable activities Fund-raising costs as a percentage of all related contributions Level of operating reserves Maintenance of the Better Business Bureau Wise Giving Certification
People	Level of satisfaction of diverse groups of employees Racial/ethnic, age, and gender diversity in recruiting new managers or staff (%)
Organizational leadership and integration	On-time strategic plan for AARP Foundation Number of members donating to the AARP Foundation Number of volunteers engaged
Social impact and value	Number (%) of Senior Community Service Employment Program (SCSEP) enrollees in unsubsidized jobs Number of Tax-Aid customers served Number (%) of new age or disability employment discrimination, pensions and employee benefits, financial fraud, grandparenting, and government or public benefits cases positively affected by the AARP policy positions

engaging AARP members, donors, volunteers, and other external constituents. Table 3.5 provides examples of performance measures in each of the four perspectives.

The types of metrics used in the AARP Foundation are very broad and include *input* measures (that is, dollars raised, costs, and so on), *process* measures (that is, maintenance of the BBB Wise Giving Certification), *output* measures (that is, on-time strategic plan), *outcome* measures (that is, level of satisfaction of diverse groups of employees), and *social impact* measures, such as the percentage of new age/disability employment discrimination, pensions and employee benefits, financial fraud, grandparenting, and government or public benefits cases positively affected by the AARP policy positions.

Summary

Increasingly, nonprofits are developing performance measurement systems to evaluate success toward achieving their missions. Combined with financial metric performance in both social impact–focused and member-focused organizations, such data allow you to have a more informed view as to actual performance against mission.

Questions the Trustee Should Ask

Effective measurement of performance against the mission is one of the thorniest challenges nonprofits are dealing with today. Best practice is still emerging. The questions a trustee should ask include the following:

- Does the organization have a defined set of metrics for measuring performance? Do I understand the metrics and the process by which they are developed?
- Does the organization have industry benchmark performance comparisons? How is the organization doing vis-à-vis others?
- Have these performance metrics been recently reviewed for appropriateness?
- Does the organization understand the potentially dysfunctional incentives that can emerge from excessive reliance on these measures? How is this being managed? Am I satisfied with this?
- Can I draw maps similar to Figures 3.2 and 3.3 for my organization? If not, why not? How can the organization start a similar process? Who should be involved?

4

FINANCIAL STRATEGY AND OVERSIGHT

Cash flow is important! It is also true the emphasis on social impact or a member focus for nonprofit organizations is critical. In Chapters Two and Three, we discussed the concerns relating to mission establishment and performance assessment measures, which are among the most important issues facing nonprofit boards. Too often we have found that boards become so focused on operating budget and funding issues that they forget the reason why the organization exists and why they have personally committed to it. The cold reality, however, is that the board has the ultimate *fiduciary responsibility* for the organization. Developing, implementing, and overseeing a coherent financial strategy are critical board functions, in addition to overseeing the organization's financial stability. In the end, without financial resources there is no mission. Conversely, all the financial resources in the world are irrelevant if not focused on a well-thought-out mission. Nonprofits, as noted earlier, do fail!

Board members generally understand the issues associated with measurement of financial performance better than they do the measurement of social performance and impact. In part this is because of the numeric processes involved in financial measurement which give a feeling of precision. This is one reason that nonprofit board members often gravitate toward financial measures—not because they are more important but rather that they are easier to understand. A second reason, of course, is that many nonprofit board members are experienced in the corporate sector; hence, focusing on financial performance is routine and comfortable, and aligns with their expertise. Thus, as was discussed in Chapter Three, we make special note that mission performance assessment, though more difficult to measure and often with a long-term horizon, is a high-priority item for the board.

Having said that, however, financial performance is critical. Without liquidity and solvency in the short and long term, the organization cannot continue the work on its mission. It should be noted that significant differences exist in the preparation and content of nonprofit financials from those of for-profits. This causes major adjustments for board members with education and experience in the corporate world, because what on the surface may seem to be good performance and appropriate liquidity on a going concern basis, may in reality be anything but.

The net income, earnings per share, and growth in market capitalization are all widely focused performance metrics and important components of long-term and short-term executive performance assessment and compensation in the for-profit world. There are literally no analogies for these items in the nonprofit world. Two financial metrics of the for-profit world, free cash flow and revenue growth, however, are very relevant to the nonprofit world. As described below, an important additional source of funds for the nonprofit world not available to the for-profit, is philanthropy in its various forms of annual giving, capital campaigns, and planned giving. Philanthropy will be extensively discussed in Chapter Five.

Overview of Nonprofit Finances

The following paragraphs are a primer of what a new nonprofit board member from a for-profit background needs to worry about as she looks at the nonprofit's financial statement.

1. *The accounting framework* for nonprofits is not normal accrual accounting, but rather its accounts are segregated and kept

track of through a series of funds. Hence it is called *fund accounting*. This is highly confusing to the moderately skilled reader of financial statements and absolute Greek to the neophyte. For six consecutive years, at the inaugural fall board meeting of one of the author's boards, the business manager would endeavor to explain fund accounting. Each year, the meeting would start in high good humor with everyone vowing to get it this year. Each year, however, after ten minutes, the first board member dropped off and by the forty-fifth minute, only the hard-core finance committee members were grimly hanging in and the rest were asleep. On the seventh year, when the board chair changed, the first thing the new chair did was to eliminate fund accounting statements for board use and instead got the business office to recast them in normal accrual format. What was given up in correctness and obscuring liquidity was offset completely by usefulness for most operating decisions.

At the core, fund accounting segments revenues and costs in a way that makes it possible to ensure compliance for the terms of all contracts and restricted gifts. It highlights which resources are available for immediate-use expenditure and which may not be used for current expenditures. To the untutored eye, an organization may appear to have ample financial resources to meet its daily operating needs. As one gains an appreciation, however, for the limitations on how these organization's financial resources can be used as a result of gift restrictions, for example, often the reality is the organization may have deep cash flow problems and great difficulty in legally meeting payroll. The reality is most nonprofits appreciate unrestricted gifts because it gives them financial flexibility; however, many donors are often attracted by very specific opportunities and don't want to give unrestricted money.

The following paragraphs give some feel for this complexity. Current funds, the most important of which is often called the operating fund, keeps track of the daily receipt of unrestricted revenues (including unrestricted gifts) and the operating expenses which may be applied against these revenues. The complexity comes when there are significant revenues that are limited by the donor (or grantor) to very specific purposes. These could be contracts, specific programs, or, in universities, gifts to specific departments. These restricted revenues can only be matched against specific costs on these contracts, programs, and departments. This leads to a multiplicity of funds that are used to ensure the appropriate matching revenues and expenses to ensure compliance with donor limitations.

A second category of funds are those related to buildings and equipment. These include funds containing assets at historic costs, funds that have been put aside for unplanned repairs and maintenance, and funds being held for specific projects in progress. As will be noted subsequently, often there is no provision for depreciation.

A third class of funds are those that keep track of endowment. The income from the various endowments (and sometimes the principal) is released to the current funds in accordance with the terms of the gift. Because these terms can vary widely, there may be great complexity as the organization tries to legally comply with the terms of the gift in a rapidly changing world. The authors have been in numerous situations where the proposed terms of a gift have been so onerous that, ultimately, the organization chose not to accept it.

The practical implications here are that a cursory reading of the financial statements may suggest the organization has plenty of cash and liquidity when it doesn't. This is also complicated by the fact that to the casual reader, transfers between funds may seem to be taking place legally in a way that may charitably be called opaque. Table 4.1 highlights some key differences between for-profit accounting and the fund accounting used in nonprofits.

**Table 4.1 Key Differences Between Corporate Accounting
and Nonprofit Accounting**

For-Profit Accounting	*Nonprofit Fund Accounting*
Matches *revenues* and *expenses* → going concern profit number	No going concern profit numbers
Balance sheet historic cost (assets, land, and physical assets) may be understated	Balance sheet historic cost (assets, land, and physical assets) may be understated
Funds flow is easy to understand Organization viability highlighted	Transfers between funds obscure organization viability
Full accrual accounting	No depreciation mandated
	Many accruals optional
	Legally mandated for gift compliance
	Highlights restrictions in redeployment of funds
Meaning of numbers generally understood by financial community	Meaning of numbers generally not comprehended by boards

2. *Depreciation* is frequently not included in the statements. This adjustment must be made by the reader to ensure that the organization is viable over the long term. It is exceedingly easy for the organization to underreach in service pricing and philanthropy efforts and, as a consequence, allow the plant and other tangible assets to gradually decay into faded elegance. When one of the authors joined the board of a struggling science museum for a short period, by the time he had walked from the entrance to the board room for the first board meeting, he knew it was dead. Its more than fifty-year-old facilities were filled with technology ten to fifteen years out of date, especially ironic for a science museum. It had suffered through twenty years of board neglect in raising funds for facilities renewal. The

accounting system had allowed them to believe they were breaking even as a going concern which, in fact, nothing could have been further from the truth. Despite an injection of $5 million in new funds and a new board, within a year the museum was bankrupt and closed. In its place today is a nice set of condos.

In the same vein, break-even cash flow is not enough on a long-term basis. A surplus must be generated from operations to facilitate maintenance and growth, and, if necessary, to provide a base to secure more debt. The authors have frequently demanded in their nonprofit statements that depreciation accounts be included for these management control reasons.

3. *Fixed assets* are not appropriately recognized in terms of their current value. Trustees of organizations that have substantial amounts of land, for example, may find that this asset is significantly undervalued, and consequently the organizations have more resources than they know about. Not long ago the chair of an organization doing roughly $7 million in revenues and losing $500,000 per year from operations before unusual gifts, faced such a demoralized board that he had to devote an entire meeting to the fact that, on the positive side, they had no debt and were sitting on $30 million of highly marketable real estate assets (which could be borrowed against in an extreme situation). The reality was that even if the board wanted to, they couldn't put the organization into bankruptcy for over ten years. Conversely, with inadequate or no depreciation in other situations (like the aforementioned science museum) assets may be grossly overvalued on the balance sheet.

4. *Quarterly numbers* do not have the same external significance as in the for-profit arena where financial markets are looking for specific profit performance. (For the nonprofit, these numbers are normally not distributed externally. For internal

control purposes, variances from budget on either revenue or expense items, on the monthly or quarterly reports for the nonprofit, however, are always a matter of concern. Similarly, progress reports indicating time slippages or cost overruns on major building and capital projects are a matter of intense concern. Unfortunately, judgment must be applied in interpreting these numbers because meeting financial goals is not always the only criterion for a project's success. Not long ago, an elementary school under intense enrollment pressure was running 10 percent over budget on a project to redo its library and the front of the school. Money was tight and there was intense pressure by the board to cut back the design of the building to something much more utilitarian to meet financial targets. After intense debate, the board ultimately came to focus on the fact that first visual impressions of the school would be critical in making it appealing to prospective parents of four-year-olds. Consequently, the overrun was approved and the original design maintained. In subsequent years, as the school's enrollment soared while other competitive schools languished, it became clear that the right decision had been made.

A decade later, no one will remember whether you made the construction budget numbers, but conversely an eyesore will grate forever. The prime example of cost overrun no doubt is the spectacular Sydney Opera House (Australia), whose original construction cost estimate was $7 million and whose final cost was over $100 million. "Big Digs" happen in the nonprofit world too.

5. *Cash flow is king!* The board must be focused on both the short run and long run. When cash is gone and there are no additional sources, the nonprofit disappears. The authors remember running a seminar fifteen years ago in a beautiful British hotel that had previously been a boarding school for

140 years before going bankrupt. Looking at the plaques on the seminar room wall listing all the head boys of the nineteenth century was very sobering. In another setting recently, one board member poignantly said to another, "This board, its energy and its personal philanthropy is the only thing standing between us and insolvency. Our sustained negative cash flows and limited hard assets will otherwise seal our fate. It is ultimately no one else's responsibility."

6. *Hidden liabilities* and unrecognized pledging of assets can be special problems for midsize organizations that have been around a long time and which may have had weak institutional memory and sloppy procedures. All involved still shudder at the memory of a struggling nonprofit in the moments after they had dismissed their CFO. After a moment's pause, the CFO reached into his briefcase and hauled out a letter, saying: "I guess this means the house I am living in is now mine." No one on the board knew that as a reward for services rendered a decade earlier, the board treasurer at the time had assigned to the CFO the title for a very expensive house deliverable to him when he departed from the organization. This development, which turned out to be legally unassailable, was a devastating blow and shock to a troubled organization. Similarly, clarity is needed to understand any legal encumbrances on assets and funds. A history of weak auditors and business managers may have left significant surprises for subsequent boards.

7. *Management of the endowment* and the rate of income withdrawal from it must be carefully examined for both prudence and long-term viability. Organizations that are fortunate enough to have endowments need several trustees with financial sophistication to oversee its management. The difference professionals can make is extraordinary. Several years ago, a national nonprofit holding company with a very sophisticated investment management

committee focused on two regional subsidiaries whose funds were not managed by the investment committee, but rather by local committees. In each case, it turned out that the total returns of the subsidiaries had lagged that of the parent by 3 to 4 percent per year over a decade. Put another way, both subsidiaries had recently launched capital campaigns which in aggregate, if successful, would not make up for the decade of poor returns on their investments. Needless to say, by trustee fiat all funds are now managed by the central investment management committee.

Endowment yield is a very complex topic, as the more you withdraw, the less is available for the future. A withdrawal rate of 4.5 percent to support operations has been a widely used industry benchmark over the years but there are wide variances in actual practice. With higher withdrawals putting the sustainability of the endowment at risk, however, trustees of organizations under financial stress are tempted to go to much larger numbers and ignore the long-term implications of their actions. These large withdrawal numbers may encourage the organization to engage in unwise expansion of activities or, instead, to imprudently delay downsizing. As a practical matter, often the endowment payout number in the annual budget is delayed one year to ensure that this revenue number is a predictable line item in the annual budget. Alternatively, the trustees may elect to pay out on a three-year rolling average so in times of turmoil in the financial markets as we saw in 2008, the organization has time to trim its operating expenses in an orderly fashion rather than taking a massive reduction of endowment payout in one quick gulp, causing the organization to undertake truly draconian cost cuts.

Endowment is a double-edged sword. No matter how much you have, your appetite is always for more money to finance more activities. The only difference in expressed need for more endowment between a local elementary day

school and Harvard University is a matter of zeroes.
However, in times of dislocation in the markets, when
endowments shrink dramatically, major programs and
initiatives of the nonprofits may have to be dramatically
curtailed, regardless of their value. A memorable moment
for the authors in 2009 was talking to a trustee of a nonprofit
who noted how fortunate they were to have almost no
endowment. While all their peer organizations were cutting
back programs and expenses in response to endowment
meltdowns, for them it was business as usual. Obviously, of
course, there was also the unspoken of vulnerability to a
collapse in operating income which happily had not
occurred for them. A final issue on endowment is how much
of it is donor restricted to purposes that may no longer be
aligned to the mission of the organization. As will be
discussed in Chapter Five, what appeals to donors today may
be irrelevant to students and scholars of a university in the
distant future (a dedicated faculty chair on textile operations
which currently exists at one business school comes to
mind). As a result of these factors, endowment may not
provide as much financial flexibility for an institution in
hard times as the board would wish.

8. *Annual giving* and capital gifts often may play a very
important role in the operations of the nonprofit. Figure 4.1,
taken from a case series on the Dana Hall School, is a
prototypical picture of the interplay among operating
income, annual giving, and capital gifts over a thirty year
time. The exhibit shows that in over twenty-six years, not
once was cash flow from operations positive (not unusual for
many nonprofits). Even when annual giving was added in,
the cash flows remained negative. When capital gifts,
foundation grants, planned gifts, and so on, however, were
added in, the picture changed. From 1980–1988, this was a
net cash flow positive generating institution as was true from
1996 to the present day. The lack of these types of gifts

Figure 4.1 1980–2005 Sources of Cash Flow for Dana Hall School[1]

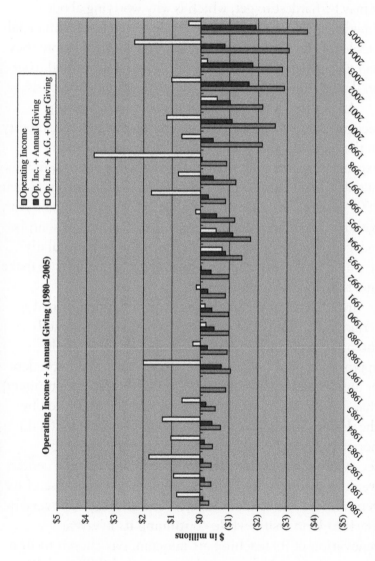

Operating Income + Annual Giving (1980–2005)

Legend:
- Operating Income
- Op. Inc. + Annual Giving
- Op. Inc. + A.G. + Other Giving

y-axis: $ in millions ($5, $4, $3, $2, $1, $0, ($1), ($2), ($3), ($4), ($5))

x-axis: 1980 1981 1982 1983 1984 1985 1986 1987 1988 1989 1990 1991 1992 1993 1994 1995 1996 1997 1998 1999 2000 2001 2002 2003 2004 2005

Note 1: Operating income excludes recognized investment gains and losses.

Note 2: Operating income includes, for years 1998–2005, annual debt payments of approximately $400k, which rose to approximately $900k in 2005 as a result of debt incurred to build the Shipley Center.

between 1988–1996 (when they really needed them), resulted in sustained cash deficits. The sobering reality is that at the time when you most need philanthropic support, it may be hardest to get, which is why worrying about liquidity is so important. Foundations often have a financial profile for the recipient institution they look for before they will give a grant. In difficult times, major donors tend to sit on the sideline and watch, thereby intensifying the crisis.

As was true for endowment payout, annual giving recognition may also be delayed one year to provide stability in the budgeting process and help to ensure that cost expansion occurs only when it is sustainable (that is, money raised in fiscal year 2008 is the number used in the fiscal year 2009 budget). For many nonprofits, 2009 was a difficult year, with income from annual giving either flattened or sharply reduced. The new board member needs to be particularly sensitive to these dynamics while reviewing budgets to make sure they reflect current reality.

In 2010, capital campaigns are also flagging in real terms and a number of construction and other capital-intensive projects have been put on hold. Previously approved capital budgets have turned out to be imprudent or unsustainable. In some cases philanthropic commitments that were made in good faith have not been honored by the donor. Similarly, anticipated but unspecified gifts do not arrive on schedule. In another example, a major secondary school's new multimillion-dollar science center went forward in spite of the funding climate because of its centrality to the school's mission and strategy. Conversely, Harvard University, while continuing its five-year renovation of its teaching art museum, has chosen to stop numerous other projects including its multibillion-dollar stem cell research center. A broad-based, knowledgeable board is critical to make these hard decisions that can delay or erode mission fulfillment.

Finally, with regard to the long term, understanding the current status of planned giving is important. Erratic to the nth degree in their arrival, these gifts can be transforming when they arrive.

9. *Debt* and its servicing status. Medium and large nonprofits have access to the public debt markets. Though tapping these markets can allow much quicker progress on facility expansion, it also brings balance sheet risk and the need to comply with various debt covenants. In prosperous times, this has allowed hospitals, for example, to embark on new programs and projects to upgrade facilities. In difficult times, such as 2001–2003, a major New England hospital group, for example, was facing major losses and had to focus a large amount of its energy to ensure it remained inside the debt service compliance limits. In these circumstances, various bond insurers and government officials can become a part of board life for a period, which is a very undesirable scenario. This part of the nonprofit scene will seem very familiar to the new trustee from the for-profit world, where organizations have failed or had to merge as a result of inability to manage this item.

10. *Auditing* is a potential vulnerability of the small nonprofit. The combination of a small audit firm (sometimes one person), a volunteer inexperienced audit chair, and a semi-experienced CFO opens the door to risk, either through fraud or incompetence. As was noted earlier, it is important to have one or two experienced financial members on the board to ensure that the normal protocols of a post Sarbanes-Oxley world are observed (bad things happen in the nonprofit world as well).

11. *Embedded for-profit activities*. Eager to raise funds, some nonprofit organizations have launched earned-income ventures and other hybrid organizational structures. Earned-income ventures relate to payments received in direct

exchange for a product, service, or privilege. They are considered for-profit activities that often support a nonprofit venture (HBS Publishing, for example, is a for-profit which is owned by nonprofit Harvard Business School). These may also be known as social entrepreneurship, social enterprise mission-based venturing, and venturepreneurship, and appear in the form of fees for service (for example, counseling, consulting, government contracts), tuition for training, leasing space, membership dues, cause-related marketing (for example, licensing or sponsorship), manufacturing and selling products, buying a franchise and buying an existing business. Examples of organizations that rely heavily on earned income include, for example, the YMCA, the Boys & Girls Clubs, the Salvation Army, and Ray and Joan Kroc Community Centers, where various products and services are provided to generate additional revenue for the organization. BRAC, the Bangladesh Rural Advancement Committee, is now the largest nonprofit organization in the world, reaching 110 million people annually through its health, education, and economic development programs. It generates 80 percent of its $485 million budget from its social enterprises. These include micro-lending institutions, craft shops, printing presses, and dairy projects.[2] In other cases, however, earned income accounts for only a small share of funding, and many of the ventures that have been launched to actually make money are unprofitable.[3] A main reason lies in an inadequate evaluation of the challenges and returns of running a business.

Financial Performance Measurement in the Nonprofit Sector

Some of the most appropriate financial performance measures that nonprofit organizations often use for the measurement and evaluation of financial performance are provided in Table 4.2.

**Table 4.2 Examples of Financial Performance
Measures of Nonprofit Organizations[4]**

Category	Performance Measures
Administrative efficiency	Administrative expenses divided by total expenses of the organization Percentage of revenues the organization spends on administrative expenses
Program efficiency	Program support or charitable commitment (% of total expenses spent directly for the charitable purpose) Program expenses divided by total expenses Program expenses growth Current spending factor (total expenses divided by total revenues) Program output index (number of units of actual physical output divided by total program expenses) Productivity rate (outputs divided by inputs)
Fund-raising efficiency	Percentage of donations left after subtracting the cost of getting them Percentage of revenues the organization spends on fund-raising expenses Fund-raising expenses divided by total expenses Donor dependency (operational surplus subtracted from donations, divided by donations)
Other financial performance measures	Revenue growth Working capital ratio (working capital divided by total expenses) Days cash in hand

However, many of them cannot be directly used for comparisons across organizations even in the same industry because of the differences in organizational missions, strategies, organizational structures, and systems. A research hospital is different from a safety net hospital. The numbers are nonetheless important for the board to think about.

Analysis of these financial performance measures provide important information on the organization's efficiency of spending the valuable resources, costs incurred, revenue growth, and how financially successful the organization is with its various programs.

For potential donors, information on financial health of nonprofit organizations is of particular importance as they think about their giving. For this reason, the Charity Navigator, a nonprofit organization founded in 2001, has become quite popular. It helps charitable givers make giving decisions by providing information on financial health of charities.[5] Charities (excluding hospitals, schools and universities, and community foundations) are evaluated based on financial information each charity provides annually in their public disclosures. Two broad areas of financial health are evaluated:

- *Organizational efficiency* is analyzed by four performance categories: program expenses divided by total operational expenses; administrative expenses divided by total operating expenses; fund-raising expenses divided by total operating expenses; and fund-raising efficiency, calculated as the charity's fund-raising expenses divided by the total contributions the charity receives as a result.
- *Organizational capacity* is analyzed by three performance categories: primary revenue growth over four years; program expenses growth over four years; and working capital ratio, calculated as working capital divided by total expenses.

Charities are scored qualitatively in each of the categories, assigned ratings in organizational efficiency and organizational capability, and finally evaluated for their overall financial health. It should be noted: the Charity Navigator does not address the program effectiveness and social impact measures. It only provides examples of financial performance measures that managers can use for evaluating their organization's financial health.

BBB Wise Giving Alliance and the Canadian Council of Christian Charities Seal of Accountability are two other organizations that provide information on financial health of charities and other nonprofit organizations. These use audited financial statements and provide a seal of approval after performing their research on audited results. The BBB Wise Giving Alliance Seal indicates that a nonprofit organization adheres to twenty standards, whereas the Canadian Council of Christian Charities Seal of Accountability indicates the charity adheres to nine high standards of ethical and operational standards. Other organizations doing this work include GuideStar, Rockefeller Philanthropy Advisors, New Philanthropy Capital, Geneva Global, Development Ratings, and GiveWell. For example, GiveWell attempts to gather and disseminate exhaustive data on the effectiveness of charities, including data on their strategies and program details.[6] The board of a nonprofit should be cognizant of how their financial health is viewed by these organizations.

Summary

Although finance remains important for nonprofit organizations because sustained losses can lead to its demise, this data must be supplemented by measures that relate to achieving mission success as suggested in Chapter Three. Most important, it should be noted that like the for-profit sector, an inappropriate selection of performance measures may enhance the possibility of unethical behavior that can lead to massive losses in terms of reputation, donations, and trust. Ethics Resource Center's national survey[7] reports that observations of fraud (doctored financial records, lying to stakeholders, and so on) are now roughly as prevalent in nonprofit organizations as they are in the for-profit sectors. Charities are losing billions of dollars to fraud, which not only impairs their current financial sustainability but also diminishes their credibility among donors and endangers their long-term achievement of mission.

Questions the Trustee Should Ask

The board has ultimate fiduciary responsibility for the organization. Key questions for the trustee:

- Does the organization have the right skills on the board to execute these responsibilities? If not, how can we recruit them?
- Does the board understand the reality of the organization's financial condition? If not, does anyone?
- Is the organization a going concern or has the lack of depreciation accounting and current value of assets obscured its real performance?
- Do I understand the organization's cash situation?
- Is the organization's debt sustainable?
- Is the organization's balance sheet and cash protected in case of an adverse economic environment (that is, when donations and fees drop sharply)?
- Do adequate transparent measures exist for the trustee to monitor the organization's efficiency and financial health?

5

PHILANTHROPY

Welcome to a different world. Nothing so differentiates the operations of the nonprofit from that of its for-profit brethren than its heavy reliance in most cases on philanthropy for major financial support. This may come in modest increments such as the local church bake sales. It may come in midsize gifts to the organization's annual fund. It may come in mega components such as major capital pledges for new wings of museums and hospitals. In many cases, these gifts are the difference between high-quality and low-quality services and, in extremis, the difference between survival or death. The sources of funds may come from individuals, foundations, corporations, or, in some cases, government agencies. Frankly, a very important part of your role as a board member is participation in these activities at least as a contributor (according to your means) and often as a solicitor and identifier of prospects and general advocate of the development function. We find it hard to conceive of a nonprofit board member who would not want to contribute something to an organization's financial support and help find additional supporters. It is an integral part of the role.

At present, this is a uniquely American phenomena. It is built deeply into its culture and facilitated by the U.S. tax code that gives very significant tax deductions for gifts to recognized charities. When the authors travel to other countries, they are struck by the frequent absence of this perspective. At a recent seminar for board members of nonprofits in Australia, the authors received considerable push back from many of the board members on this item. It was explained that this was "not the way we do things here," and that it was inappropriate to ask a board member for money. It is quite enough that members devote their time to the board. The discussion was lively and intense, and ultimately lead to an article in a local philanthropic journal to more fully make the case for why board members should help to financially support their organizations. We should add that the operating heads of the Australia nonprofits were overwhelmingly in favor of the American model.

Our contention is that philanthropy is a major responsibility of the board and the CEO. With respect to the board, it is captured in the following three time-honored phrases.

Give, Get, Get Off!
Work, Wealth, Wisdom
Time, Talent, Treasure

Each of these phrases captures a different potential grouping of responsibilities for a board member, with the common link being the role of personal financial commitments and solicitations. In short, an important role of the board member is helping to secure funds for the organization so that it may pursue its mission. This can happen in many ways.

The Development Organization—Securing Funds

An integral part of most nonprofits is the development organization (it may vary from one person to a cast of hundreds). Development is responsible for securing philanthropic funds for the organization and managing the various donors at different stages of their engagement with the nonprofit.

Personal Gifts

As noted above, the authors believe that each board member should be able to make a commitment consistent with his or her financial resources. Several very important caveats need to be made in this regard. As time passes and an individual grows more deeply committed to the mission, the amount one is willing to give often grows dramatically. Repeatedly, we have seen initial $1,000 gifts evolve over time (years) into $1 million gifts or more as particular aspects of an organization's mission come to appeal particularly to an individual.

Different people have very different capacities for giving. A friend of the authors noted that during her period as a chair of a community service operation for battered women, she valued the $25 contribution from an unemployed parent of two, who very effectively represented the service to the local communities, as much as she did the $100,000 pledge from a business owner. Each financially contributed according to his or her abilities and both were very effective trustees in every sense of the word. A trustee who as a matter of principle does not want to give, however, is a liability that must be dealt with. Many potential donors to a nonprofit expect as a matter of course that all trustees will have personally given money to the organization. If this is not the case, it diminishes the effectiveness of their solicitation.

Foundations

Foundations can be an enormous source of support for nonprofits. In 2009 the roughly 75,000 grant-making foundations gave grants totaling nearly $43 billion. Nearly 75 percent of the grants came from independent or family foundations with the rest coming from corporate and community foundations.[1] Board members can be enormously helpful in identifying potential foundations by facilitating introductions and otherwise assisting in the granting process. Though enormously helpful, many foundations like to focus their giving on the launching of new services with the expectation that the organization will then find permanent funding. This needs to be thought through by the CEO and board before accepting the funds. The core question is whether the organization can raise money to support the new level of activity on an ongoing basis, or whether the funding will create an unwieldy overhead structure that will only have to be dismantled in the future. Some foundations may be off limits to the struggling nonprofit because they demand a positive cash flow from operations for several years before making a grant (the authors walked through a difficult situation when a potentially life-saving grant for an organization was denied on this basis). This was another example of when you don't need money, plenty is available—but when you do need it, none is available. For the rest of this chapter we will treat foundations as a special type of donor.

Identifying and Approaching Potential Donors

The trustees are the eyes and ears of the board in identifying people who may care deeply about the cause, or are susceptible to being approached. We offer two examples. Some years ago, a friend of one of the authors approached him to say his child was applying to a school and asked what the author thought were the chances of the child getting in. The author joked it probably depended on whether the child had inherited the caller's genes (the answer being no) or that of his spouse (the answer being yes). When the call was ended, the author went to the school's head and reported the call. He noted the call had come from one of the most genuine caring philanthropists in the community, who had a penchant for getting deeply involved in things with his children. The author, however, had no recommendation as he had no insight into the abilities of the child, or whether the school was a good fit. These were decisions and judgments which lay in the province of the CEO and the admissions department. Fortunately, the child turned out to have great ability and was admitted. The friend joined the board the following year and in subsequent periods became cochair of its capital campaign and a truly significant donor (and the child graduated with high honors).

In another case, over a period of years, a patient received extraordinary care from a health organization. Through his personal relationships with a trustee over several years, the patient ultimately made the health organization a major beneficiary of his estate, which dramatically enabled an expansion of the health care organization. Trustees are often an organization's best ambassadors.

Hosting Events

For friends and neighbors, these community and regular events attended by the CEO are an important way of extending contacts and making new friends as well as deepening the engagement of the hosts. As will be noted later, for larger nonprofits, the research staff is critical in both identifying potential prospects to host and to be invited to these events and in providing clues on how to start a conversation. The authors have repeatedly found a single item (such as a child's college or a sport interest) in a three-page research report invaluable in starting a solicitation discussion on a more personal basis.

Participating in Direct Solicitations

For some individuals, asking other people for support is hard. A friend of one the authors noted that his wife and mother were united in the belief that nice people don't ask other people for money. The friend was able to rise above that training! One of the real benefits to an organization when you as a trustee personally ask someone for money is that it deepens your own commitment and understanding of the organization and its mission. Implicitly, in making the case for someone else to give money, you wind up asking yourself, "Have I really given enough?" Very often a trustee realizes that the answer is no. The authors have often thought that one of the great benefits of the two-year missions that young Mormons take to recruit new members for the church is that in the process of trying to directly solicit new members for the church, they wind up dramatically increasing their own attachment, which usually lasts a lifetime. In the end, the increased commitment of the solicitor may be equally or more important than his or her effectiveness as a solicitor.

In short, participating and helping to lead philanthropic activities is a very important part of being a nonprofit trustee. It is, of course, also a very important part of the nonprofit CEO's job, who is often a trustee as well. Potential donors want to hear firsthand from the CEO about her vision of the organization's mission and, specifically, what she would like their gift to accomplish. A good rule of thumb is that in normal times, 50 percent of a nonprofit CEO's time is consumed in development activities. At times of major capital campaigns, this can rise to the majority of the CEO's time (often, the smaller the organization, the more time a CEO spends on solicitation). Big gifts take large amounts of time. For example, soliciting the largest gift in a recent university capital campaign required the CEO to make over seventeen out-of-town trips and dinners with the donor before securing the gift. In this context, during the time of a major capital campaign, CEO continuity is critical. In a real way donors are betting on the CEO to execute their vision of the gift's objectives. When, for example, Tom Gerrity stepped down as head of Trinity College in Hartford, Connecticut, two months before the public phase of their new capital campaign was to be unveiled, this resulted in the campaign being delayed for three years. Similarly, Larry Summers's departure from Harvard indefinitely postponed what had been a rapidly coalescing capital campaign.

The Development Organization–Donor Life Cycle

The previous paragraphs have focused on the critical role of the trustees and the CEO in executing philanthropy. The reality, however, is that this is only one part of the development iceberg for the midsize and larger organization. Repeatedly, it turns out that the existence of a highly professional development department is key to an organization's philanthropic success. The following paragraphs talk about the main elements of what this department should include. Three points, however, must be noted at the beginning. First, to raise money you have to spend money. Unfortunately, often a ramp-up in expenditures can precede revenue growth for a significant period of time during the launch phase. This can make an organization that is building its capacity appear to be inefficient in its use of fund-raising dollars as opposed to one which is in a steady state. Nonetheless, development expenditures as a percentage of gifts raised must be monitored carefully and compared to industry standards. Second, continuity of relationships and structures are really important for development work. Development officers with long tenure in an organization are a real asset as they provide crucial trust and continuity with past and future donors. Also key is the ability to facilitate the development of deep donor relationships with professionals in the organization such as curators (for museums), professors (for colleges), social workers (for community centers), and so forth. These personal ties of potential donors to the individuals charged with mission execution helps fund-raising enormously. Fund-raising at its best is a relationship between a donor and an organization that in many cases lasts for a lifetime, perhaps only concluding in a planned gift at the time of the donor's death. Third, because of inevitable staff turnover, good records are very important. Multiple conversations with a donor over time realistically often take place across two or more solicitors. Inadequate organizational memory can be devastating in terms of losing touch on important information about an individual. Recently a multimillion-dollar prospect was well along the way to making a major naming gift, when a long-term employee who was not in the soliciting loop half-remembered a conversation he had had over lunch three years earlier with a retired staff member. Following up with the retired staff member, his recollection was confirmed that the "hot" prospect had spent three years in an overseas jail for theft. Incredible embarrassment would have occurred had this gift been consummated.

Donor Identification

Philanthropy begins with donor identification, a very complex process with approaches varying widely by type of organization. Educational institutions, for example, usually have names and addresses of alumni and past and current parents who are potential donors. The trick is how to learn about them in terms of their interests, current capacity to give, and overall philanthropic profile. First and easiest are the self-nominated, who regularly give to the annual fund. Very often, however, these are only the surface fish and the real potential is hidden much deeper in the ocean. Half-day rating sessions of classmates and other parents may be very helpful in a school context. Often, these rating sessions are imperfect because over the years an individual's circumstances can dramatically change. One of the authors remembers participating in his undergraduate class rating sessions for his twenty-fifth reunion. All classmates were rated and each assigned to one of four giving potential categories. These were over $500,000, $100,000 to 500,000, $25,000 to $100,000, and other smaller amounts. When the reunion campaign was actually completed several years late and the (highly successful) campaign was over, the names initially identified for the over $500,000 category had turned out to be largely correct. All the other names were mostly wrong, reflecting the circumstances of the individual's family situation twenty-five years earlier, and had no relationship to their current financial position. Fortunately, balancing this was a large unnoticed group of classmates who, unbeknownst to their classmates, had been quietly building highly successful careers. They came to the forefront and completely filled the gaps in the upper donor categories.

In today's world, a professional research group is very useful in trolling Google, and a variety of donor databases, looking for matches with its lists of members. In addition, broad-based one-on-one conversations with key peers are a good source of relevant prospects. As a practical matter, the authors find that the longer a brainstorming conversation goes on the longer the list of meaningful names produced. Consequently, these conversations should not be hurried, as it takes time for names to swim back into one's memory through a variety of associations.

This information then becomes raw material for invitee lists to cultivation events, where trustees and professional staff can reach out to get to know them better and assess their interest and potential giving capacity. This often leads to individuals being asked to join advisory boards to further deepen their involvement and interest in the organization. In a number of states, for example, many nonprofits have a body called the corporation. This is a group of 50 to 150 people who meet annually (or quarterly) to be briefed on the key events affecting the institution, elect a predetermined list of trustees, and to socialize. These bodies can help the organization gain clarity into key community issues through the insights of these individuals. The members in turn, by participating in these discussions, often deepen their commitment to the organization by more fully understanding its mission and challenges. In many cases, it is from this group that future trustees and major donors are recruited.

Another example of using activities to enhance the organization's development is Boston's Museum of Fine Arts. For over thirty years it has had a guide's committee whose members are recruited from all over the metropolitan region. Each year thirty new guides are trained over a four-month period in various aspects of the museum's activities. They are then moved into appropriate volunteer activities in the museum for four years. This committee has been a highly successful magnet in recruiting individuals into the museum's orbit from particular demographics. These demographics embrace individuals whose children have recently left home for college, individuals who have demonstrated community philanthropic interest, and those who are now in a position to rebalance their time and interest as well as broaden their philanthropic involvement. It has turned to be a very effective way to attract future and present collectors, supporters, and even trustees.

Donor Research and File Maintenance

This is a crucial activity. For example, in the case of schools and universities, it is key to maintain giving records going all the way back to date of graduation. This information is then supplemented over the years with records of conversations that highlight individual concerns about the institution, their perceived interests, and other discussion points which are relevant in shaping solicitation plans. For example, in a university setting, such records are critical because almost surely the administrators handling the class's fifth reunion will be different than those handling the tenth reunion and beyond.

A note of caution must be raised about giving records. Over time people's interests and capabilities can sharply change. The authors vividly remember a conversation twenty years ago, when a major potential donor specifically asked not to be solicited for a particular set of activities in a university. This was adhered to for fifteen years and in turn helped solidify his commitment to another series of activities in the university. When his daughter unexpectedly decided to attend the university, however, this was deemed to be an event that should cause previous solicitation embargoes to be lifted, and they were lifted with great success. People often do change their views and priorities over a lifetime.

Hospitals pose a particularly challenging situation because many of its potentially strongest advocates are grateful patients, parents of patients, spouses of patients, or children of patients. Because of legitimate privacy concerns, much of this medical information must be kept confidential in the doctors' files and away from solicitors. Identifying your real supporters is a challenge for a hospital's development staff. Word of mouth, informed referrals, and neighborhood gatherings are some ways of working around this constraint and making contact with these individuals.

Social cause organizations wind up relying heavily on word-of-mouth networks and friends as they try to develop their lists. It is a very time-consuming process to develop and manage these lists, but it is absolutely crucial for development success. Similarly, the back office function of updating addresses, telephone numbers, bios, and other records are an essential part of the development operation.

Donor Cultivation

This is as much an art as a science. The most important concept, however, is recognition that philanthropy at the core is a *relational* not a *transactional* activity. Any individual donor gift is something to be truly celebrated and the donor must be appropriately thanked. If the donor contact is well managed, however, this often is simply an initial step in a lifelong relationship of giving and support. As described above, donor identification can happen in many ways. Developing and maintaining the relationship over the decades can unfold in many ways. Some of the approaches are the following:

- *Regular written contact.* These may be in the form of alumni bulletins, class notes, newsletters, and the like.
- *E-mail updates on key activities and Web site access are a more modern approach.* These are tools to help maintain donor contact with the nonprofit through communicating important events of potential interest to the donor in the organization. To reach younger donors, the new technologies are becoming a primary approach. Older donors, however, often prefer the traditional written approach. The over-seventy set mostly does not yet take the

computer onto their bed in the evening, but they will take the alumni magazine.

- *Invitation to special events*. These events are well staffed by appropriate people including trustees, long-term supporters of the organization, and relevant professional staff and are built around substantive activities like lectures, exhibitions, and so on. The task of the event is to excite the participants' interest in the organization and identify those to follow up with. It is truly amazing what can be learned in a cocktail conversation.

- *Personal visits*. Special events are followed by one-on-one visits of development staff to start cultivating donors by getting to know them personally and learn about their interests. These conversations are a delicate minuet of both finding out donor interests and highlighting for them areas of potential need for the organization. These conversations require a great deal of sensitivity and listening because often there is a wide gap between the two lists at the beginning.

Donor Ask

All the preceding activities are designed to lead to this task. It can take place in as little as a few months or as long as a decade. One of the most successful efforts in the authors' experience was a relationship effort that only culminated at the end of fifteen years. In changed personal circumstances, when asked to consider a certain number, the donor's response was to propose a number four times larger.

The ask is the culmination of research, developing a relationship with the donor (and often also their spouse), and formulation of a well-architected proposal. For large gifts in relation to the organization, normally the ask will be made by the CEO, building on their personal relationship. Trustee and other solicitations are usually best done in groups of two. This is to help ensure the solicitor doesn't equivocate in asking for the agreed-on amount. A trustee on his own often loses the courage to ask the agreed-on number. A team of two dramatically reduces the likelihood of this occurrence.

An important reality is that few people are insulted if you ask for more than their interest and capacity. If you underask, the donors will act with alacrity, simultaneously making the pledge and congratulating themselves for having gotten off lightly. The authors ruefully remember several of these occasions with the donor much later happily admitting he got off for a lot less than he expected.

Even if the donor has received poor treatment at the hands of an organization, the donor may still feel an attachment. A memorable event was a chair's description of fund-raising for a small school. In the chair's judgment, in the previous year the school had inappropriately rejected the three-year-old grandson of a trustee. In the early stages of a capital campaign for a new library for the school, all trustees of the school had been personally solicited by the chair except this one. The chair was too embarrassed to do so. One night he received a call from the trustee, obliquely expressing a desire to be solicited. In her living room the following week, after the presentation was over, the grandmother hesitated for five seconds. Then, with a glint in her eye, she said, "this project will outlast the current head," reached for her checkbook, and promptly wrote out a five-figure gift (the school the grandchild ultimately went to got a new building). Nothing ventured, nothing gained. In another situation, a major corporate CEO had felt wronged by his alma mater. The school's CEO flew five and a half hours to the corporate headquarters for an appointment with the alumnus. After he was left cooling his heels for three hours, he was told the CEO was unavailable. It took him another five and a half hours to fly home. The happy ending was that at the urging of a classmate, the (ultimately embarrassed) CEO sent a $400,000 check four years later (while in the meantime providing an institution-naming gift for a competing school).

Realistically, the first time the ask is made, it is relatively unusual for immediate agreement to be reached. Even if the concept is appealing, myriad details remain to be resolved, even though the donor may have nearly made up her mind. Often the donor wants a tightly restricted-use gift. Two problems of an enduring nature exist with restricted gifts. The first is the donor's desires may not tightly align with those of the organization. It can be a long, complex process to negotiate this. In some cases, the institution wisely decides it cannot live with this type of restriction and has to end the dialogue. Disappointing though this is, it is a lot better than taking the money, failing to deliver, and having to return it in a hail of ill will and unsavory publicity. The second problem is that the gift may be worded for something appropriate for today's world but possibly not for tomorrow's. From the institution's viewpoint, the more flexibility that can be left for long-term interpretation of the spirit of the gift, the better.

Discussion of naming opportunities is another area of delicacy. This needs to be formulated in a policy statement so that scarce naming opportunities are not given away at too low a price. On the opposite extreme there is another group that craves privacy. They want to be philanthropic but not draw attention to themselves. We are often surprised how many six- or seven-figure gifts are then listed in annual donor lists under the category of anonymous or in the $10,000 category. Finally, it should be noted that until a signed letter is received, there is always a possibility of the deal falling through.

Donor Stewardship

This is a very sensitive and important part of the donor management process following the first gift. The first and most important step is to ensure the donor's intent is being filled and that she knows it. For example, if the gift is a scholarship, sending an annual thank-you letter or introducing the donor to the actual recipient of the scholarship at an event can be very powerful tools. Good chemistry from these encounters can sometimes produce additional fellowships or other forms of support. One university, for example, solicits money for fellowships that must be spent completely in five years. Ideally, the donors will be so pleased with the results that at the next five-year reunion they will give another equal or greater amount again to be completely spent down in the next five years (so far, this program has been very successful). In another case, money was given for part of a major building. The donor was put on the design committee. Over the course of two years, he participated in the vibrancy of the design battles, the frustration of the permitting process, and the consequently infuriating redesigns that had to occur. Completely absorbed and involved, his original gift ultimately rose by 300 percent to help the organization deal with those issues. A happy story, but this could have worked out differently.

Great care is needed in the area of stewardship because over time the organization's needs and those of the donor both change. The purpose for which the original gift was given may no longer be an institutionally important one; the needs of society and the institution may have moved on to other areas. A dialogue with the donor effectively maintained over time can often help this restructuring to take place. Absent the dialogue, the request may fail. This is an intensely delicate affair and, if mismanaged, could in the extreme lead to the return of funds— sometimes under very embarrassing legal pressure.

At the same time, during the process of stewardship, the donor's interests may have shifted. Someone once interested in art may now be more interested in medical technology, perhaps as a result of a child's illness. The ability to pick up on this can result in future conversations leading to additional gifts in this new area, possibly culminating in a "planned gift" (that is, money received at the time of the donor's death). The key word for development, as mentioned earlier, is always "relational." Too often the coauthors have seen an excessive focus on today's gift have an unfavorable impact on what would ideally be a very long-term relationship with a donor.

The Development Organization Structure

The previous paragraphs have focused on the critical role of the trustee in the development function and the donor life cycle. The development organization is in place to support these two activities. Depending on the size of the organization, the staff may be as small as one person or number in the hundreds. Regardless of the size there are a number of functions that must be performed, each of which will be described below.

The typical development organization is divided into two parts, namely the askers and the supporters. Each is equally important. The supporters create the ambiance and environment, the ocean in which the askers can fish. The two organizations are staffed by very different types of people. As noted earlier, the askers tend to be highly personable, disciplined, guileful, and capable of making the ask. The supporters are also very personable (a requirement for being in development), disciplined, and organized, but their spines often turn to jelly at the thought of actually asking someone for money. To a remarkable degree those that are good askers often are not so good supporters and vice versa.

The aim of the supporters is to give high-quality undifferentiated support to all. The wisdom of this is critical. The authors still remember a phone call from the head of an annual fund on a Thursday, to see if a half hour could be spent the next day with a couple returning for their thirtieth reunion. The total lifetime giving of the couple to the institution over thirty years had been, to date, $262. They had attended every reunion of their class and were on no special target donor list. They had also just called the annual fund head to see if she was the right person to whom they should give their $500,000 check.

The meeting the next day was very educational. The couple explained that after graduating from school (which, they noted, had been a very happy part of their life and included the births of their two children), they had founded a small privately held company whose growth had consumed all their spare cash. Six months earlier they had sold the company and for the first time in their lives they were liquid. Crediting their experience at the school with the company's success, they wanted to send a thank-you gift. It was a very happy half hour, the story of which has been endlessly repeated by the authors to numerous audiences. You never know who is in the group, and the only safe strategy we have found is to treat all members at a gathering in exactly the same way. This is why one group runs the actual events and another group runs the fund-raising. Church and state are clearly separate. Since this gift took place the authors have heard numerous similar stories.

The Askers

These are the people at the sharp end of the development chain who actually do the direct work with the donors. In small organizations one person, such as the CEO, may do the entire function, whereas in the larger organization a highly specialized and segmented set of roles may exist. They may be broadly categorized into two groups: those associated with the annual fund and those with capital or major gifts. The role and staffing of each is quite different.

Annual Fund

At the core of most organizations philanthropic activity is the annual fund to which, it is hoped, donors will give to on a regular basis hopefully in ever-increasing amounts. The annual fund is usually executed by a combination of direct mail or, more recently, e-mail appeals, backed up by personal calls from staff or from volunteers recruited by and organized by the staff. The key to a successful annual campaign include the following.

- Accurate *donor lists* with up-to-date addresses and records of past giving. The written and telephonic ask will be at the previous level or ideally a higher one. Telephonic asks for the most part are vastly superior in effectiveness.

- A series of *recognition* levels and societies which enable solicitors to help ratchet up individual giving so one can move to a higher recognition level. The importance of these recognition levels may be reinforced by special dinners or receptions. A matter of development discipline is increasing the level for participation in each society every few years (this is important in an inflationary world).

- Less savory is the deliberate soliciting for the annual fund every three or four months hoping donors may either be generous and deliberately give a second time or more likely give again by mistake. Following four gifts in a year to the local public TV channel one of the author's wives now has a sophisticated weekly tracking system to prevent recurrence of this. Her hostility to their past practices has solidified her view that the annual pledge should not be increased.

- A *disciplined follow-up process* to target nonrespondents. A personal call to these people from a friend or acquaintance, however, is likely to be much more effective than one from a professional solicitor. Many people hesitate to disappoint a classmate, fellow parent, or friend. However, they feel no compunction about stiffing someone they don't know. Done near calendar year end and fiscal year end, telethons are an effective way to bring an annual fund to its goals.

- Active *recruiting of volunteers* and setting up a positive environment for them to make their calls. Success breeds success in the telecommunications boiler room.

- Waves of *information materials* to keep a fresh message in the minds of donors. In the spirit of recent political campaigns it is a lot easier to do this in the interconnected world of e-mail.

- *Setting and managing goals* for both participation and total giving helps add an air of urgency and discipline to the process. Comparison against other groups helps harness one's competitive instincts.

- *Discipline and focus* as opposed to donor interpersonal communication skills are the most critical skills for the annual fund staff to possess. Skills in attracting and exciting the right group of volunteers is also key.

Planning

Careful planning and staging of program tasks months in advance is critical, including time at the end for a last-minute blitz to put the program over the top. Sadly, visible deadlines are very important in motivating activity.

Major Gifts

Askers for major gifts and capital gifts have a very different challenge. The task here is primarily a long-drawn-out, highly individualized process. In every sense, their time horizon, execution, and skill level are different from those involved in the annual fund. The first step for the major gift asker is the identification of the prospect list. Potential names come from a variety of sources. Among the most common as noted earlier are

- Major givers to the annual fund. The tension between the annual fund and major gift officers is intense. In general, major gift officers have priority, although in educational institutions their gifts are also included in class totals for reunion campaigns.

- Word-of-mouth reference from reliable sources such as classmates, community leaders, and so on.

- Analysis of research databases tracking philanthropic gifts and cross classifying with people who have links to the organization.

- Major gifts given to other organizations (uncovered by research)
- Individuals whose organizations have recently had great economic success and might be expected to have received significant bonuses or stock options.

As noted earlier, the next step for the major gifts officer is to begin a process of stimulating the prospective donor to become more actively interested in the organizations and its mission. This normally begins with a personal visit in the donor's home or office. If the meeting is successful, in addition to a thank-you note, the officer could

- Recommend an appointment to a special advisory board which might meet one or more times a year. Although the members of this committee are appropriately valued for their advice, equally or more important they are also being educated on the mission and values of the organization, and in so doing ideally will find their interest and commitment deepening in ways that will ultimately increase their philanthropic support.
- Offer an invitation to a special event to learn more about the organization and its current issues. Ultimately this could lead to a special meeting with the CEO or another high-ranking individual who can share both insights and their passion for the organization. This meeting would be preceded by a meeting with the development officer where the main objective would be to cultivate the prospect's receptivity to the CEO meeting. A second objective of this meeting, which is more subtle, is structuring a conversation to help reveal which aspect of the organization's mission might be of particular interest to the individual and which she might be interested in supporting. This produces a minuet which can last several years as the middle ground between the individual's and organization's interests is explored and,

ideally, a shared intersect can be found. This is a very delicate process, because often there is a very wide divergence of interests and sometimes despite good faith it is impossible to bridge the gap. Often the temptation on the part of an organization is to take the money at hand and hope for success. As noted earlier, this can lead to disastrous results and very unfortunate publicity. In another vein, it should be noted that there is an enormous temptation for a development officer to urge that naming rights for a $40 million building go for $10 million rather than pushing hard to get the gift up to $40 million. The manager of development and the CEO are responsible for making sure this does not happen. The toughest situation the authors have experienced was when the naming rights for a $50 million project were given for $10 million and thus fatally wounded the development effort by capping other gifts. It is very hard to get your money back once you have given the project away too cheaply.

For modest projects, the special gifts officer may be able to handle the project from beginning to end, but more often their role is that of a setup person for a line officer who will then make the actual sale. The major gifts officer is then subsequently responsible for following up and executing all the details and making sure the project does not become derailed.

The Supporters

What are the ingredients of a good support infrastructure? We believe there are at least six, although for small organizations they may be grouped together in various different configurations.

General Sustained Outreach. This includes a large variety of written and electronic communications. Traditional media include alumni bulletins with customized class notes, monthly newsletters, and an aggressive public relations and news media effort. More modern approaches include well-crafted Web sites, targeted e-mailing, special topical podcasts across the Web. Each of these by definition affects all constituencies the same way. As a general observation triggered by Barack Obama's great success in his presidential campaign, the long-term trend is to move away from print media toward various electronic media. Given, however, that a significant part of philanthropy comes from the over-the-hill crowd (ten years older than whatever your age is), however, progress is gradual in this area as far as dollars raised if in not numbers of people using the technology.

Community Events. These events, open to everyone, or to those who pay a special fee, provide a high-quality social and professional experience for all who attend. Such events are intended to provide an ambient environment within which a lot of meaningful networking between administrators, development professionals, and potential donors can take place, when the institution is sold or presented in a very attractive way. In the afterglow of these events, the tone has been struck for both professional and amateur askers to do their thing. For school reunion events, class experts and the organizational professionals can combine to deliver truly meaningful experiences. Although it is hard to cost justify any specific event, the collective impact can change the context of potential donors' relationship to the organization. It is, however, a complicated long-term relationship. Running these events can be very logistically taxing and larger development organizations have special departments for this.

Clubs. Medium and large organizations can have alumni clubs around the world. Professionals from the organization on business trips are encouraged to stop by the local club and give an evening speech. Again, the ambiance of these events reminds alumni of their organization and its mission. The events hopefully leave positive vibrations in the minds of the attendees. Measuring cost-effectiveness is hard because the clubs add value in so many ways. Of course, depending on the quality of local leadership, the effectiveness will vary widely. One of the coauthors was stunned to see a small fourteen-person local club effortlessly (apparently) host a three-day conference for seven hundred attendees halfway around the world from the organization's headquarters. The event energized an important part of the alumni base in ways that were inconceivable in advance, and in later years the effort paid real dividends. Conversely their largest club completely failed in a similar effort. A matter of leadership! Again, large development organizations have staff to guide clubs and supporter groups of various types in such ways as providing speakers and support materials, furnishing standard software, giving policy guidance on using the organization's name, helping to get started, and so forth.

Special Advisory Boards. Selected out of the general pool of supporters to provide special advice, those groups can play a critical role in the organization's development activities. For the most part, members add value through a combination of their ability to give good advice and the possibility of their being co-opted into deeper financial engagement with the organization. The planning and delivery of special advisory board meetings are done by professional event planning staff with no fund-raising component at all. From museums to social welfare organizations to hospitals, this has turned out to be a highly effective approach. In order to maximize the utility of the boards, they tend to be largish, about forty to sixty people, have ample time built in for discussion (highly senior people prefer talking over listening), and have term limits to gracefully enable the sustained introduction of new individuals. Again, it is the uniformity of high-quality care across all the advisory boards that is critical; to do this right requires both staff and money.

Special Events. In addition to the normal annual rhythm of community events, five-year reunions, and advisory boards, episodic events are planned to involve constituents and, ideally, to deepen their engagement. Examples of this type of event include groundbreaking and dedication of new buildings, centennial celebrations, and dedication of a new chair or lecture series. In addition, the development support staff may team with volunteers to help facilitate the organization's charity balls, and so forth.

Research. This is one of the most important functions of development support. It is charged with three tasks. The first is to make informed estimates of potential donors' total assets, potential giving interest, and their liquidity. There are a wide variety of external databases and search engines to help facilitate this. These are very helpful but also somewhat imperfect tools which are best placed in the hands of a creative researcher. Nonetheless, it is impressive what can be discovered from the public record about potential donors' stock options, other holdings of stock, and real estate values. The second task of research is to provide a broad smattering of background personal data (number of children, colleges attended, and so on), which can provide a springboard for finding a shared interest between the development staff, the asker, and the potential donor. Less than 5 percent of this information is ultimately useful, but finding a single shared interest between a solicitor and donor can go a long way to facilitate building a bond between the two from the beginning. A single shared common interest point was all a successful solicitor looked for to spark an early discussion between him and the potential donor. Time after time he would find that tiny nugget in a research report. Most vividly he remembers finding a joint college in common among their children, a topic that triggered a warm discussion in what ultimately turned out several visits later to be a successful multimillion-dollar gift. Finally, through analysis of past gifts, research may give insight into the values and interests of the donor which can help form ideas as to what kind of a gift might be sought.

Stewardship

Special attention needs to be paid to ensuring that donors' terms of gift are adhered to and that they are regularly informed about the uses of their funds. This communication is critical both to ensure that intent is fulfilled as well as to lay the foundation for future asks. Also important, stewardship builds a climate of trust between the donor and the organization, such that if the organization's needs dramatically change, there is a possibility of a sympathetic consideration by the donor of a modification of the terms of gift. Approaches of stewardship can include

- Annual status report on the use of the funds
- Letters from recipients of scholarships to the donor
- Invitation to special events on-site to visit facilities given by the donor
- Regular visits by officers and development staff to keep the donor apprised of the institution's progress
- Meticulous records of these activities that are critical to ensure that a donor doesn't get lost in the cracks, which can easily happen over decades as staff and leadership of the organization change

A head of a large development organization recently noted that when he assumed his responsibilities it was the value of the stewardship group that he was most skeptical about. Five years later, as a result of a series of colorful incidents and near misses, he saw it as his most valuable.

Back Office

Throughout the chapter, we have referred to the importance of detailed record keeping. In the information age all but the very smallest organization has a computerized record system, almost always built around one or more software packages. Key functions include

- Complete name and address files of donors, their personal background data, giving history, and, increasingly, reports of visits.
- Ability to change records online as people move, trip reports from visits come in, and so on.
- Receiving, recording, and acknowledgment of all gifts in a timely fashion. This includes getting checks into the bank and money collected from credit card gifts. This is particularly complicated for gifts of stocks, real estate, and various forms of tangible properties which require assessments of value to be made by the organization for tax purposes. Getting the donor right is also key. Mistakenly crediting a gift to a donor's ex-spouse does not build strong donor relations.
- The coordination of mailings (both U.S. mail and e-mail) from design through to actual delivery.
- Posting of comments from constituents (such as alumni) and checking to make sure they are in the zone. A particularly embarrassing incident was a practical joke played on an investment banker alum of an institution who, according to "his" letter (sent by someone else), had become a barefoot begging monk in Kashmir (he had not).
- Preparation of Web site and donor gift recognition mailings, carefully noting all donor restrictions on publicity.

The least glamorous part of support, the back office is nonetheless absolutely vital and real donor problems emerge when it is not well done. Running it is a nightmare because of the huge seasonal fluctuations in activity. Usually a disproportionate amount of gifts come at either calendar year end or fiscal year end. Establishing the cutoff dates for recognition of these gifts is very difficult because of the pressure to meet campaign goals ("just give me another two days").

Summary

A few final summary comments for a trustee to take into account:

1. Development askers are very special people. Organized and extroverted by nature, they need the ability to handle disappointment and require lots of positive day-to-day reinforcement from their leaders and trustees. The number of rejections they receive each day in the course of the job significantly exceeds the number of successes. It requires psychologically robust people to deal with the rejection of the ask, particularly when the process of cultivation has taken place over a long period of time. To be effective, they have to be close to the operational and strategic challenges of the institution and have a close working relationship with the most senior staff, including trustees. It is very important that managers and trustees be aware of the stress involved in these jobs and provide appropriate reinforcement. Often managers in other parts of the organization have very little respect for or understanding of the skills and challenges of the asker's job, frequently criticizing the size of the budget and the absence of immediate results.

2. Development is best thought of as a long-term revenue center as opposed to a short-term cost center. Under management pressure it is easy to cut costs to meet annual budget targets but difficult and time-consuming to build long-term relationships. It is even harder to assess performance of development annually because of the often very long time lag between the beginning of the soliciting effort and the eventual success. One of the most important gifts with which the authors have been

involved, which ultimately raised several tens of millions of dollars, was the result of a fifteen-year process of engagement with literally no intermediate tangible results. Six years later an even larger gift emerged from the same donor. Modern accounting is not up to this type of time frame.

3. It is critical to get the development staff close to the leadership and mission of the organization (not easy where both time and office space are at a premium). Development staff's effectiveness crucially depends on their ability to internalize the values of the organization and understand who, depending on the circumstances, are the right members of the organization to put in front of potential donors. A remotely located development office with the loose mandate to just raise money is unlikely to be successful. A central function that has close access to both senior staff and their thinking is much more likely to succeed. This point is often not recognized by the rest of the organization who feel resentful about development's privileged status and compensation levels.

4. One reality is that the CEO is critical to development. For new CEOs it often takes time to get the knack of doing development activities. Where possible, it is helpful for the development staff to begin by scheduling a couple of highly likely early big wins for the CEO. At the same time, because cultivation can take a long time, a new CEO needs to start very early meeting major donor prospects. This is hard because the new CEO is usually under intense pressure, as she takes over the reins of the organization, to focus on internal operations. This leaves the development people chafing at the bit to get her in the field. Realistically, however, for the new CEO, early priority must go to taking charge and understanding the existing organization, and working on operational issues.

Without this base and understanding there is nothing to sell. However, as early as four to nine months into the job, development begins to take more priority.

In addition, it is very important to tailor the approach to the CEO's personality and strengths. Some CEOs are good at giving speeches to large groups of people. Others may not be so good at that but are terrific at striking up one-on-one conversations and establishing instant rapport with individuals. Others excel in small-group discussions while still others do a wonderful job on the golf course. The reality is that most CEOs will have to do all of the above (except golf) but substantial advantage comes from allocating more time to the activities that they are good at and less to those activities they are not so good at. This will make them much more likely to be productive. Finally, recognizing and managing the reality of the CEO's ability to handle fatigue is critical. In one organization the CEO was exceptionally effective, when rested, in one-on-one sessions—and he liked to do eight to ten sessions per day. The reality, however, was that his energy and effectiveness dropped dramatically over the course of a day. His staff ultimately managed a calendar which ensured that there would be lots of last-minute cancellations, so he was forced to rest. Each CEO has her strengths and weaknesses and the challenge is to use limited development time in the most efficient way.

5. It is extremely useful for number 2s and 3s in command in an organization to go on some fund-raising calls. Direct participation in such calls helps them understand how hard it is and how much planning is needed. Equally important, it helps them builds empathy for this part of the CEO's role. Most important, it helps them understand what the CEO is doing during his physical absence from the organization.

Questions the Trustee Should Ask

Philanthropy is at the heart of the viability and mission-fulfilling capabilities of many nonprofits. Key questions for the trustee:

- Is the board development oriented? Is the organization itself development oriented?

- Have I made an appropriate contribution to the organization, both in giving and asking?

- How do the organization's development results stack up against those of similar organizations? Why are they different? If results are low, what can be done about it?

- Is the CEO's life structured to play the critical development role she should?

- Is the organization thinking about long-term cultivation and not just short-term giving?

- Does the organization remember to ask and not just cultivate?

- Is the organization appropriately staffed for its long-term development needs and not cutting corners?

6

BOARD STRUCTURE AND ROLE

Very excited to make your first contribution to society as a nonprofit board member, you have just finished talking to the head of the governance committee and two other trustees you slightly know, have picked up a cup of coffee, and found a seat, which is likely to be the one you will use for your entire tenure on the board. Looking out, you see twenty-five other trustees, plus six to eight staff members, all with name tags on their lapels and small name plates in front of them, none of which you can read. Some of the officers like the CEO and head of finance, you are pretty sure what they do. Others, like head of development and head of medical affairs, you haven't a clue what their roles are. You are familiar with other corporate roles, such as head of marketing and sales, but these are conspicuous by their absence.

The first agenda item is a review of the state of the industry, and the organization's position in it. Filled with acronyms and ideas you never heard of, the entire presentation is both opaque and mysterious. This is followed by an interesting update by the president and CEO, which is a bit confusing because there is also someone called the chairman, who you thought was in charge, but really isn't—or is she? A series of committee chairs make presentations (you never knew a board could have so many committees), including one from the ominously titled Capital Campaign Feasibility Study Sub-Committee. The board meeting concludes in executive session (with all staff members and the CEO gone). Maybe the chairman is in charge after all. A shadow group called the executive committee (apparently a big deal) talked about their activities since the last meeting. Finally a report is presented by the compensation committee on the results of a board and staff survey on satisfaction with the CEO plus a consultant's survey of competitor salary practice and a recommended salary for the CEO for the next year (it turns out these people make a lot of money).

In preparation for the meeting, you had received an inch-and-a-half-thick binder filled with minutes of previous meetings, committee reports, financial results year to date, and several interesting papers concerning trends in the industry. The variances looked small but what was their capital fund and the transfer to the operating fund all about?

Over morning coffee, you met the chief financial officer who talked about how glad he is to have a financially savvy trustee who can understand the implications of long-term negative cash flows (you must have missed something in reading the numbers). You also met a warm, gregarious person called head of development, who informed you that you were on the development committee and he very much wanted to meet you in your office the next week.

In short, you've just experienced a bewildering first meeting with lots of new faces, an overload of acronyms, and a sinking feeling in the pit of your stomach as to what exactly you have gotten into.

This is not an atypical story and it's one that could have been managed a lot better! In this chapter, we will pick up from this point and introduce the functions and issues of the nonprofit board, its various subcommittees, and how they play out over time.

A multiple possible set of forces brought you to join the board. Those could include passion about the cause the nonprofit is focused on, previous direct interaction with it in some way, personal acquaintance with several trustees, and so on. In any event, you were brought to the attention of the board's governance committee, which is responsible for the board's composition, structure, and processes, and for assessment of its performance. At the outset it is critical to understand the broad duties of the board.

The Roles and Responsibilities of the Board

At the most fundamental level there are standards of conduct that directors must meet in fulfilling their responsibilities. These responsibilities are typically defined in the organization's bylaws, in numerous statutes and regulations, and in court precedents. Directors' duties have often been broadly described as the duty of care, the duty of loyalty, and the duty of obedience. The *duty of care* refers to the diligence and skill that must be exercised when a member makes a decision as a steward of the organization, while the *duty of loyalty* means that members must subordinate their personal interests to those of the organization, avoiding all possible conflicts of interest. Finally, the *duty of obedience* requires that members must obey the law and ensure that the organization itself complies with the law.

Though management is responsible for managing organizations on a day-to-day basis, boards of directors assume a central role in governance as their primary duty is to promote the long-term interests of the organization. Over time, there have been changes in the definition of the roles and responsibilities of boards. Generally, though, the board assumes three core responsibilities:

- Oversight of mission and mission development processes
- Accountability for mission performance and financial sustainability
- Evaluating performance of senior staff

To execute the responsibilities for all but the smallest organization the board is normally divided into a series of committees where much of the board work is done. The most important of these committees is the governance committee.

Governance Committee

Figure 6.1 presents a schematic of the key tasks of the governance committee. Effectively done, it is the most important

Figure 6.1 Determinants of Board Performance[1]

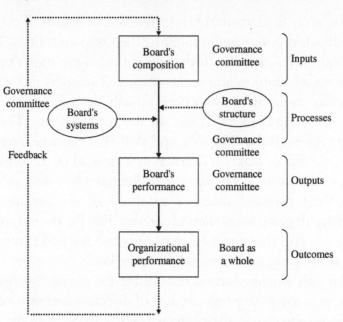

committee of the board. Its first task is exercising a broad view of the organization's challenges and mission to identify and attract the right group of individuals to the board. As will be discussed, this is a very complex process requiring time horizons of a decade or more. The second task is to manage the staffing of standing committees of the board, the board leadership and its succession, as well as provide input to the staffing of the ad hoc committees. It is responsible for facilitating the assessment of board performance and of individual members, and for initiating corrective programs as necessary. Finally, it must assess whether the Board has the right mix of skills on it. The effective execution of these tasks is essential to increasing confidence in the organization and its operations by various constituencies such as donors, staff, and community.

Repeatedly failures of boards result from having the wrong mix of skills on the board, inattention to recruiting people for the various leadership roles that must be filled in the future, and poor processes for monitoring the organization's climate and relationships between the board and permanent staff. This committee normally includes some of the most experienced trustees on the board, plus those who have the ability to network broadly in the relevant communities. This is critical, because except for the largest national and international nonprofits, professional search firms are not used (as they commonly are in the for-profit world) for trustee searches.

As noted earlier, a multiyear planning time horizon of five or more years is needed for the governance committee to do its job effectively. In the normal scheme of things, the remarkable group of people who are board leaders today will have gone on to other phases of their career five years from now, and a new and ideally well-trained group will be in place. We remember clearly the case of a major community services organization that had their five former and current board chairs compose an executive committee which held all critical decisions to itself. It had worked well for a long time and no one challenged this state of affairs. Then the combination of a changing economic environment, two deaths, and two out-of-state retirements decimated the board leadership team in a period of eight months. A group of young, relatively inexperienced trustees were suddenly thrust into tasks, whose nature and complexity they were not familiar with, and they made a lot of mistakes. It was entirely avoidable.

Potential board chairs, potential chairs of the finance committee, and so on must be brought along in appropriate developmental assignments. Because of the dynamic nature of the board composition and industry challenges, on an annual or at least a biennial basis, the committee needs to facilitate both a board and chair effectiveness evaluation. Featuring inputs anonymously from all board members and key staff, this survey is invaluable in surfacing emerging and latent issues (including inadequacies of board membership and succession) in such a way that they can be dealt with before the situation gets out of control. The findings of this evaluation must be played back to the board at an executive session where there is time to really deal with the issues (making it part of the annual board retreat is a good way to do this). The topic is sufficiently important that it should not be grafted on the end of an already crowded agenda. It takes time to assimilate and talk these issues through. As the situation warrants, written evaluations may be supplemented by telephonic interviews to uncover and probe particularly sensitive issues. In extreme cases, this may lead to the formation of an ad hoc governance process committee to study in totality the entire range of governance issues and make specific recommendations.

Discussion between the board chair or governance committee chair and each potential trustee before they join the board is critical. This discussion will identify the expectations of the new trustee along a variety of dimensions including attendance and financial support. This discussion needs to then be combined with a formal board orientation program which includes meeting key staff, provision of detailed financial and other data about the organization, as well as review of the mission statement and strategic plan (if one exists).

Though a governance committee may aspire to a situation where all trustees play an equally active role, the reality is different, as evidenced by a couple of examples.

The head of one of the legislative branches of a state was elected to a hospital board. Although he was pleased to be on the board, because of intense time pressures he almost never attended a meeting. However, anytime a health legislative or political issue came up, he was always immediately and constructively available by telephone to the hospital CEO for advice and in several cases was influential in shaping legislation in a way advantageous to the hospital. In the board chair's view, he was one of his four or five most important trustees although half the board would not recognize him if they ran into him on the street. The legislator also took great personal pride in his membership.

A similar case occurred in a large metropolitan museum where, through personal efforts by the board chair and the CEO, an avid collector and philanthropist was recruited to the board. Her annual attendance level was well below 50 percent and much of her advice when she came to a meeting would not be classified as constructive. As a result of this engagement, however, her interest in the museum as both a place for part of her personal collection to rest and as an institution to financially support grew dramatically.

It should be noted that the nonprofit board can be a remarkable source of free labor and experience. Individuals whom the organization could never afford to hire are often pleased and flattered to be asked to participate as volunteers. Examples of this include the professional money managers happy to serve on investment committees, sophisticated financial executives happy to serve on the audit and budgeting committee, and technology gurus heading ad hoc technology review committees. Others bring great marketing expertise, wide networks in important communities, and time to help in mission-critical activities like fund-raising. Particularly in the case of the small organization (but true for all) the board is a remarkable source of free labor and perspective. Critically for the small organization, energy, charisma, and passion for the mission makes the CEO an indispensable person in helping attract those individuals.

These examples help explain why nonprofit boards can become large, attendance levels can be well below 100 percent, and yet in the bigger picture, this may be OK. An experienced governance committee can fully balance these issues and make these assessments.

When recruiting the board member, it is important that the organization's term-limit policies be explained to the individual. It is terribly easy to allow a board to grow gracefully old and inbred, and lose contact with its key communities. Term limits are important to get new blood to the board. Because of the board's philanthropic role, term limits are much more important to the nonprofit. One of the most intriguing assignments the authors recently had was reviewing a board that included four trustees, all over eighty years old, each of whom had served for more than forty years. Not surprisingly, the interviews with these four senior trustees as to what the organization was going to look like a decade in the future was of less interest to them since they did not expect to be active. As a result of the review, three of them are now trustee emeritus and their places are filled by energetic leaders of the next generation. It is also important to have several officer positions and other slots like "head of corporation," which can be filled on an annual basis. This allows a few people to be retained beyond normal retirement who either provide useful organizational memory or are seen as candidates for playing future leadership roles. In general, however, term limits are critical in ensuring a steady flow of new people to the board, thus bringing new energy and perspective.

Very few people are insulted by being asked to join a board (even if they don't accept). The process of leaving a board, however, is much more fraught with difficulty and must be dealt with from the very beginning if ill-will is not to ensue at the end of one's service. Often, as part of the last one to two years on the board, membership on the governance committee can be an important part of the graceful disengagement process. Helping the nonprofit to think through its future board needs and participate actively in building the future board in many cases has been very effective in helping people to gracefully step off the board and yet be willing to continue to engage the organization in another way.

In trying to put a slate of candidates together, key topics that the committee must grapple with include the following:

- Appropriate age distribution for the type of organization.
- Appropriate geographic spread to help facilitate mission execution.
- Balance of specialists related to mission versus mission generalists. In some states, for example, by law no more than

25 percent of a hospital's board can be doctors. This is to ensure community representation.

- Amount of development prospects that can be accommodated.

- Ensuring that there are no real or perceived conflicts of interest between any trustee and the organization that could trigger embarrassing publicity.

- Ensuring that an appropriate number of people with financial skills are recruited to cover the key committees in that area. A general financial literacy requirement has to apply for the budget, investment, and audit committees.

- General ability to work nondisruptively as a member of a group.

- No spousal empowerment issues with the organization that would be exacerbated by the appointment of an individual to the board.

- Clear understanding of the potential chemistry issues between the individual and the CEO. Different organizations have very different views on the importance of this issue, given their particular circumstances.

These are complex issues for which there are no easy solutions. Successful resolution over time helps build and continue strong board support and leadership of the organization. Conversely, inattention to these issues can put the entire organization at risk. Twice the authors have seen inattention to these issues create disaster. In one case, the board grew so far from the organization and its values that only the replacement of the board chair and the establishment of a special board-staff relations committee composed of three board members and three staff members prevented the recognition of a staff union and its attendant complexities. In the other case, the board dithered so long about replacing a long-term (but now out-of-steam) CEO that the organization nearly disappeared in a sea of red ink.

Additional Board Committees

If your first year on the board seems heavily focused on orientation and demonstrating good citizenship, the following years
will have an increasingly important contribution role. If in fact
you are seen as a substantial contributor, very quickly your personal time management will become an issue. In this regard, you
will quickly discover that for medium and large organizations
most of the heavy lifting is done in committees, with the main
board meetings focused on only a few key issues and hearing
committee reports.

Committees come in three types: standing committees, ad
hoc committees, and the executive committee. The following
sections discuss the principal committees insofar as their roles,
membership, and specific challenges are concerned. This section
will conclude with those things that must be done by the board
as a whole.

Standing Committees

The most time-consuming of the committees, and second only
in importance to the governance committee, is the finance committee and its associated committees of audit and investment
management (if the organization is lucky enough to have an
endowment).

Finance Committee

For a variety of reasons enumerated below, this committee is
even more important than is the mandated audit committee in
the for-profit world. In the broadest sense, this committee is responsible for reviewing and preparing the annual budget, monitoring the organization's financial performance throughout the
year, ensuring that necessary steps are taken to maintain the organization's short- and medium-term liquidity, as well as ensuring that a knowledgeable long-range financial plan and strategy

are in place. This is a huge set of responsibilities and their effective execution is critical. It is one of the reasons why financially
literate trustees are so valued.

The complexity of the task is immense because of the need
to balance mission-related issues with the realities of the organization's financial constraints. Often the core mission of the organization is profoundly cash flow negative with the resulting
enormous tension regarding how to mitigate these challenges. A
ham-handed approach of unenlightened expense cutting, for
example, can fatally destroy the organization's ability to execute
on its mission.

For example, the authors studied a college preparatory
school that had been truly struggling financially for over a decade. The school's incoming board chair, an experienced large-
company CEO, was adamant in his recommendations to deal
with the financial challenges. Double the size of all classes, eliminate all advanced placement courses, and reduce foreign language offerings from five to one. Admirable in terms of cost
reduction, it was ultimately concluded by the CEO and the
board that this approach would so weaken mission execution
that students would flee the school, revenues would plunge, and
the organization could quickly fail. A more nuanced long-
drawn-out process ultimately turned out to be the right approach. Unfortunately, the immediate departure of the chair
had to be part of the solution. Repeatedly, the phrase mentioned
earlier comes up: "Don't let the financial tail wag the mission
dog." This is where for-profit executives face their greatest challenge and why they must be mission savvy. Fundamentally
bottom-line oriented, they can be stampeded into precipitate
action by a nervous business manager. As noted in Chapter
One, in the long run cash flows must net out positive, or you are
gone. In the short and medium term, however, you have much
more financial flexibility in nonprofit organizations.

Having said this and noting the issue of mission, the reality
is that business-oriented finance committee members can bring

great strength to the organization. Many have much deeper experience in cash flow management of complex organizations than does the organization's business manager. They have often also seen these issues play out in a multiplicity of organizations.

This work is very time-consuming and very detail oriented. Two of the most effective finance chairs the coauthors know are currently retired MBAs who each had a decade of experience in finance, control, and investing before becoming full-time home-makers (each had three children at home). They could not work 8:00 AM to 8:00 PM, but with the skills from this earlier part of their lives, they brought needed professionalism (and a lot of time) to the oversight of the financial function.

The sheer complexity of this work often forces the special-ization of financial oversight functions into a variety of finance subcommittees. The more important of these are discussed in the following sections.

Investment Committee

The investment committee's job is to bring the best thinking to the management of its portfolio of stock and bonds, real estate, and so forth, and to appropriately balance risk and return. The approach varies widely depending on the size of the portfolio. For example, the management of Harvard University's portfolio is balanced between internal managers (highly compensated) and external managers (not infrequently former employees of Harvard who are even more highly compensated). A major mu-seum has six or seven highly experienced money managers on its investment committee which, on an entirely uncompensated ba-sis, allocates the resources among different asset class managers. They continually monitor performance, dropping low performers and reallocating among categories as the markets change. Boston's Beth Israel/Deaconess Hospital's Board of Managers manages the $500 million portfolio of three hospitals. Made up of extremely gifted money managers, the ten individuals donate their time to this philanthropic effort effectively (as, among other things, no money was allocated by them to Bernie Madoff). Smaller organizations (who have some endowment) do not have access to these skills and investment vehicles, and have to work with more traditional financial instruments with significantly lower returns.

Only the largest nonprofits try to manage the portfolio in-house. Consequently, the ability to attract investment professionals to a nonprofit board, as the Beth Israel/Deaconess Hospital did, can pay big dividends. Even taking into account the meltdown of the markets in 2008–2009, these professional money managers have done much better than well-meaning amateurs. Smaller organizations, however, often simply cannot attract these skilled investment volunteers to their boards to prudently advise on these kinds of investments. Consequently they must settle for a lower risk and return structure.

Financial Resources/Planning

This may be either an ad hoc or standing committee. It is responsible for developing a five- to ten-year view of the organization's need for financial resources and identifying plans for how they will be secured. If it is an ad hoc committee, it is frequently supported by outside consultants, often as preplanning for what ultimately becomes a capital campaign feasibility study. Financially oriented board members are particularly useful here to make sure that key assumptions shaping the analysis are surfaced and understood. This type of long-range financial resource planning often culminates in a board retreat, where alternate scenarios of the future are debated and decisions made. A particularly memorable situation for the authors was a long-drawn-out, meticulously prepared plan for an organization which painfully highlighted that there would never be room for the organization to physically grow in their location. In addition, for a variety of reasons, moving the location was a practical impossibility. Given that its size would be fixed, the committee then focused hard on the maintenance and growth of service quality. This ultimately led to a capital campaign to raise resources for staff salaries (a core competence of the organization which they did not want to lose) and extra financial support for certain types of clientele. Mission, financial resource constraints, and limits of growth all led to a conclusion that, though not obvious at the beginning, was the appropriate choice. At each step this discussion was guided by financially sophisticated but mission-sensitive board members. The toughest challenge that the organization's board members with for-profit backgrounds had to deal with was the reality of the mission-imposed limits to growth. They were not used to dealing with this and the discussions were heated and painful.

Audit Committee

This committee's work is focused on the annual audit and the assurance that appropriate internal financial controls are in place for the organization. In principle, this should be familiar territory to the for-profit executive. In practice, there is some real challenge because the big four accounting firms do not practice extensively in the small and midsize nonprofits. The consequence is that nonprofits are both audited by less sophisticated accountants and also tend to have a much looser internal control structure. Weak documentation and other informal processes increase the likelihood of something going wrong. Unfortunately, a nice social mission does not deter the hiring of unsavory people, or the possibility of nice people under personal financial pressure succumbing to temptation. The financial background of members of this committee is important as they need to be particularly vigilant in sniffing out potential irregularities.

Beyond the subcommittees associated with finance (investment, financial resources and planning, and audit) there are several other critical committees which are described in the following sections.

Development Committee

The third most common standing committee beyond the governance committee and finance committee is the development committee, which is responsible, along with the development director and the development office, for devising and soliciting philanthropic strategies. In a real way, of course, development is part of the role of every board member. As was discussed in Chapter Five, "Give, Get, Get Off!" resonates powerfully with reality. It is hard to think of a nonprofit board member not giving to the organization something in accordance with their means. Always critical, in a time of a capital campaign this committee's workload becomes so significant that often a special campaign steering committee is spun off to handle first the planning and then the execution of the campaign. The development committee is broadly defined as being responsible for creating and overseeing the execution of the organization's development program, which is handled by professional staff. Often a significant number of the committee members are capable of making significant gifts to the organization (they are on the committee to get a sense of the scope of giving and become comfortable in expanding their own generosity). Others support the fundraising effort by donating significant amounts of time through hosting dinners, speaking at fund-raising events, and undertaking personal solicitations. Doing each of these activities often increases one's personal generosity. The development committee members are some of the most important high-profile fund-raising ambassadors for the organization.

These roles lead to the following summary observations about the development committee:

- The committee should be large in number to optimize outcomes. Indeed, in some organizations they have morphed into three or more committees to optimize philanthropy while keeping the number of people in the room manageable.

- The meetings of the committee should have a significant component of educating the participants on current goals, progress towards goals, and broad organization priorities so that the participants can be good ambassadors. These meetings must be as upbeat as possible.
- The committee members are an important source of identifying new potential donors and providing updates on current friends whose personal circumstances have changed their giving capacity.
- The members are donors and people who are comfortable asking for support. Both the organization's development leaders of today and those of the future should be on this committee.
- Because of their very active development role, the members of this committee have particularly close relationships with the development staff.
- Extensive service on this committee is often a cause of trustee burnout.

In short, the development committee is a set of ambassadors who help to shape and guide the organization's development activities.

Physical Facilities Committee

For organizations with substantial physical assets (such as museums and colleges) this committee is where a trustee from an engineering and construction background can provide real value, saving a lot of project management fees. Responsible for the overall maintenance of facilities and the oversight of major construction projects, the workload can be enormous and the contribution invaluable.

Mission-Related Performance Committee

This group is charged with understanding the organization's mission and how well it is being executed. This is incredibly sensitive and important work. It is sensitive because it operates on the edge of what the board is directly responsible for, and what the staff feels is their responsibility. When this committee begins to look at quality of medical service in hospitals, or quality and breadth of offerings in educational institutions, or type of collections in a museum, great anxiety can arise on the part of staff as they perceive board amateurs meddling in the realm of experts. Particularly interpersonally sensitive board members are needed to handle these issues. On the other hand, when the board as a whole—either on its own initiative or because of outside pressures—takes up the topic of mission execution (often in a crisis), it is very helpful to have a subset of trustees who are knowledgeable and up to date both on these issues and who have good relationships with key staff. They can help reassure the rest of the board. In this circumstance, the committee becomes a safety net for ensuring good board performance.

The committee's membership is often a combination of very senior and very junior trustees. The very senior trustees are there to make sure the discussion does not go off the rails. The junior ones are there as part of their training to be effective trustees. This is a committee the CEO needs to stay close to. Problems coming out of this committee on either the staff or trustee side have the potential to rapidly escalate out of control. To help keep the discussion on track, if an outside expert in the field's subject matter is on the board, this is an excellent committee for that person to be assigned to. The danger of local wisdom being too narrow on an issue is always possible. Consequently, benefit can come from local viewpoints tempered by a knowledgeable outside perspective. To be effective this outside board member must have the confidence of the CEO or it will not work. The coauthors have repeatedly seen the right outside expert in the industry positively shape board dialogue because of his or her ability to generate trust of the other trustees.

Ad Hoc Committees

Ad hoc committees can be created to deal with important special issues as they come up. A couple of examples illustrate this. A community service head felt vibrations from various segments of the community that a part of their offerings were deeply deficient and out of step with the times. They had not been modernized by the staff specialists for a variety of reasons. At an appropriate time at the combined suggestion of the board chair and CEO, a blue-ribbon committee headed by a trustee and staffed by outside subject experts and several staff was convened to explore this part of the offerings. Nine months later, a dramatic new set of offerings emerged and after substantial discussion was rolled out over a multiyear period as funding sources were found. The implementation was led by the staff, and once the committee's work of conceiving a new offering was completed, it quietly faded away.

In another setting, the CEO and senior executive committee of a medical institution became alarmed at dramatic new organizational alignments of competitors in its area. An ad hoc committee led by two trustees and composed of other trustees and medical staff was set up to evaluate the continued validity and viability of their institution's mission. Assisted by outside consultants and the staff of the institution, seven months later they concluded that the institution's mission, although worthy, was no longer viable and suggested that they set off in an entirely different direction, which was ultimately done. A decade later several trustees of that early era noted in their professional judgment that, without that correction, the institution would not have survived.

When the problem has been dealt with, the ad hoc committee's role is over. Other examples of these committees include a "financial planning scenario" committee, a "curriculum review" committee, an "ad hoc ethics standards" committee, CEO search committee, and so forth; the list is endless. At the farthest extreme, to keep its 130 trustees busy and involved, Dana Farber has twenty-one committees of its board. These ad hoc committees can be tremendously demanding of both trustee and staff time. Consequently, both the chair and CEO must concur that this is a good use of scarce trustee resources before launching another committee.

Executive Committee

As noted in Chapter One, as the board grows in size, it becomes increasingly cumbersome. Unlike the now typical corporate board of six to ten members, for reasons described earlier, nonprofit boards can grow to twenty-five or more. The difficulties of these large boards are legion in number. A few of these include:

- It takes a very long time to discuss an issue and bring it to resolution. The number of people who feel they have to talk before the board can decide on an issue tends to make meetings very slow and inefficient.
- Potentially indiscreet. The larger the number of people involved, the more likely it is that sensitive and confidential information will be leaked.
- Hard to assemble in an emergency (even in the world of e-mail and instant connectivity).
- Increased likelihood of people being out of the loop through missed meetings, resulting in their having imperfect information.
- Danger of dominant personalities seizing the agenda and crowding the others out.

These pressures all lead to the need for a small, empowered group to make both sensitive decisions as well as expedient ones between meetings. Unless carefully handled, however, this can have pernicious second-order effects, creating what can be called upstairs-downstairs boards. Almost no one resents being asked into the inner sanctum. Once there; however, almost subconsciously they begin to radiate a sense of specialness and create alienation from the nonmembers. In fact, in the extreme, the executive committee may have such a good time that they don't feel it necessary to come to the board meetings. In one particularly egregious case, a friend of one of the authors was on a board two years before spotting one particularly elusive executive committee member at a board meeting. This doesn't work. Executive committee members need to have almost perfect attendance at board meetings. The appropriate roles of these committees include

- Doing routine business between regular board meetings and reporting what they have done to the next meeting of the full board.
- Identifying when an issue is of such importance that a special telephonic board meeting is needed, perhaps followed up with a special meeting. This could be as a result of a fire, criminal act by an employee, gross abuse of an employee, and so on. When in doubt, it is better to hold the special meeting, attended by counsel if appropriate.
- Reviewing CEO performance evaluation and compensation and presenting it in executive session of the board. Though this may appear threatening to the CEO, the ultimate consequences of not doing it are more so.
- Receiving reports of very sensitive information relating to misbehavior, lawsuits, and the like. In the normal course these reports may have to be presented to the board. This is a murky area, because sometimes a sensitive situation occurs which can be averted without involving the full board. Indeed, getting the broader group involved may make the incident a self-fulfilling event. This was the thinking used by a college board chair when the president first told him that

he was thinking of resigning and going to a competitor. The chair only involved one other member in the discussion to try to keep the news contained. He feared a broad-based discussion would mobilize a significant number of board members against the president on grounds of disloyalty, and make his departure inevitable, which, it turned out, it was.

• A sounding board for the CEO between meetings.

The dangers of an executive committee is that over time it can tend to gather more power unto itself and may wind up briefing the full board (and getting their inputs) less and less. They can create substantial dissatisfaction and alienation of the nonexecutive committee board members, leading at the extreme to their resignation or to a coup. Even worse, when a crisis (that the executive committee tried to contain) explodes into full view, angry and ill-informed other board members may bring less than dispassionate judgment to bear. In short, the coauthors see the executive committee as a necessary evil which must be carefully managed.

Board Meetings

There are a series of issues beyond the committee meetings that relate to the board meetings themselves and the behavior of board members. This is a complex subject. For a variety of not easily solved reasons, nonprofit board meetings tend to be longer, much more unstructured, and more poorly attended than those of for-profits. Insofar as erratic attendance is concerned, the first thing to note is that unlike for-profit boards, attendance is not a matter of public record or scrutiny. Only your fellow board members know this data. There are three reasons why erratic attendance happens. First, some board members are appointed for very specific and narrow purposes. One of the most useful board members on an education institution's board was the president of the state senate of the state where the school was located. A cursory study of the minutes would note that he only attended two board meetings in six years. When, however, the school needed special enabling legislation to close a road going through its premises and effectively increasing its athletic field space by 40 percent, he sponsored a special bill that passed through the legislation with no controversy and little discussion. He was a truly invaluable board member.

Another reason for poor attendance is the addition of trustees who are seen as potentially very large donors to the nonprofit. Sometimes these trustees decide to miss January board meetings in the snow and instead go to their winter houses in some tropical environment. It pays to have empathy for this perspective for the financial good of the organization. This means you have to be careful to not assign them to heavy workload committees like finance or governance. A third reason for poor attendance are schedule conflicts which, because of the lack of publicity about nonattendance and no meeting compensation, individuals don't try as hard to reschedule. It is up to the board chair and head of the governance committee to monitor these situations and to have whatever counseling conversations are appropriate. Key additional items about board meetings are detailed in the following paragraphs.

Social Contact

The board that knows each other well often performs better in a crisis. The dinners and receptions around a board meeting are very important activities in enabling people to get to know each other and build these critical social networks. There are also opportunities to build relationships with staff. An annual retreat accomplishes much the same thing. These retreats on an annual or at most biennial basis are a critical way of assimilating new board members into the culture and building a richer, deeper relationship between board members. Many important things can be said in an informal one-on-one coffee break conversation or late-night snack that are not so easily said in the full formality of a board meeting.

Meeting Structure

Timing needs to be articulated in advance and reasonably followed, to create an atmosphere of responsibility and respect for everyone's time. Sensitive topics need to come up earlier in the meeting when most people are at the top of their form and not when they are rushing to another engagement or catching a plane. The authors still painfully remember a board meeting that began at 8:00 PM after the annual meeting of the nonprofit organization (which had been preceded by a wine-and-cheese reception). Meant to be two hours in length, at 9:45 PM the CEO's annual evaluation and compensation came up for discussion and resolution. This was a mistake. At 1:45 AM the meeting finally broke up in angry knots of individuals milling around the parking lot venting steam. As a result of this experience, the authors vowed never again to chair a meeting lasting past 10:00 PM, a rule they have adhered to for thirty years. You simply gavel it shut and carry the agenda to the next meeting (next day telephonic if necessary). The other benefit is that once the rules are known it is easier to manage the discussion, because often the majority of the board members want an immediate resolution that day. There are physical boundaries beyond which civility begins to decay.

Meeting Content

The agenda of the meeting must be informative and emotionally engaging. CEO evaluation, compensation issues, adding or deleting an important programmatic initiative or reviewing major changes to the organization's financial position are all ingredients for a good meeting. Conversely, deadly dull monotone presentations of unexciting material that could have been read in advance are a sure way to ensure poor meeting attendance. Whenever possible there should be one or two important action-item discussions which, after debate, require a vote. Those things dramatically improve board member attendance and morale. Their scarce time is being used wisely.

Meeting Discipline

The chair needs to keep control of the meeting both to ensure there is broad participation and also see that certain individuals don't hijack the meeting with endless monologues. It is critical to manage the time devoted to formal reports and briefings. The new or insecure CEO, afraid of open discussion, may try to have every minute filled with presentations so that there is no time left for debate. This approach invariably leads to substantial dissatisfaction by board members. Our experience is that no more than 25 percent of a meeting should be devoted to presentations and the rest devoted for discussion (which often produces important insights). An appropriately organized set of briefing materials sent in advance helps facilitate this happening. In the world of e-mail and secure Web sites like Board Vantage (www.boardvantage.com) this is easy to do. Mundane, but also important, is a board book containing pictures and bios of trustees and key staff. This helps you learn and remember names. The chair calling on people for their opinion who have not participated in a meeting is also a way of helping people become engaged. None of this is rocket science but collectively these ideas help create positive face-to-face ambience in the meetings and satisfaction by the participants.

Board's Performance

As noted in Figure 6.1, assessment of how the board is performing is a key task normally assigned to the governance committee. In addition, in times of turbulence a special ad hoc committee may be set up to review all governance processes (recently successfully done in a large community services organization as a result of failures of existing processes) or even with the aid of an outside consulting organization. A more regular process is

1. An annual assessment of each committee written by the committee members. These assessments are then reviewed in totality by the committee as a whole and then by the governance committee. Alternatively a telephone survey of each member may be done by the chair of the governance committee.

2. An assessment of the board's performance as a whole by the governance committee. This may be based on either written or telephone survey. This is then reviewed in executive session of the board.

3. An assessment of individual members' performance on a formal basis, recommended by many people, and used in many for-profit corporations, which turns out in practice to be very complicated because of the volunteer nature of the board, the widely differing jobs many individuals are recruited for, and the issues of collegiality. Consequently these issues tend to be raised at the time when a term is expiring and the question of reappointment must be addressed. This is one of the reasons why term limits are so important. They provide a graceful and dignified way for something that isn't quite working out to end (this is particularly critical because of the ongoing development needs of the organization).

A nonprofit's board and its structure is truly different from the for-profit. Exhibit 6.1 is a list of characteristics that make superior for-profit board governance. As the previous pages note, this list is not a 100 percent fit with for-profit governance. To wit:

- *Independence.* For development reasons and staff relations reasons, a number of exceptions are often made in nonprofits.

Exhibit 6.1. Keys to Superior Board Performance[2]

Board Members

- Independence
- Add value

- Ethics
- Diligence

Board Processes

- Appropriate committee structure
- Productive meetings
- Effective mission and financial performance evaluation systems
- Appropriate information availability to board
- Effective succession planning
- Open communication and reporting systems between board, CEO, and staff

---

- *Adds value.* Nonprofit needs a very broad portfolio of skills including philanthropic support. This is hard to pin down explicitly.
- *Ethics.* High standards needed in both cases.
- *Diligence.* For development reasons this is not needed for the whole nonprofit board but you do need a hard-working core.
- *Committee structure.* Many more committees are needed for nonprofit.
- *Productive meetings.* High standards needed for both but harder to achieve in nonprofit.
- *Effective mission and financial performance evaluation systems.* High standards desired for both.
- *Information availability to board.* High need for both. Table 6.1 is a list of information that should be made available to the nonprofit board.

- *Effective succession planning.* For many nonprofits the reality is an outside search.

- *Open communication and reporting system between board, CEO, and staff.* High standards desired for both.

Table 6.1 A Sample of Strategic Information Required for Nonprofit Boards[3]

Topic	Minimum Frequency
Board Information for Accountability	
Financial statements	Quarterly
Reports or updates on critical accounting policies, judgments, and alternative treatments	Annual
Reports from external auditors (quality of the audit process or internal controls and issues raised during audit)	Quarterly
Reports on complaints received	Annual
Reports on major risk exposure	Quarterly
Report on regulatory compliance	Quarterly
Reports on current significant litigation	As required
Reports on board's performance	Annual
Board Information for Senior-Level Staffing and Performance Evaluation	
Report on compensation policy, including performance targets and objectives (CEO and top executives)	Annual
Benchmarking report; executive compensation package	Annual
Report of succession planning	Annual
Report on staff development activities	Annual
Report on fund-raising	Quarterly
Report on board performance	Annual
Board Information for Strategic Oversight	
Budgets	Annual
Five-year strategic plan	Annual

(continued)

Table 6.1   (*Continued*)

Topic	Minimum Frequency
Report on major capital expenditures, acquisitions, and divestitures	As required
Annual strategic plan	Annual
Operating plans (major supporting initiatives)	Quarterly
Any alternate strategies considered and rejected	Annual
Reports on major policies/management systems and organizational structure	Annual
Progress report on strategic plan; reports on operating variances (deviation/shortcomings from original plan)	Quarterly
Reports on financial performance (for every major segment)	Quarterly
Reports on operating performance (for example, productivity or quality data) for every major segment	Quarterly

Exhibit 6.2 contains a more detailed list of questions that are helpful for a trustee to ask in getting insights as to how well the board is performing.

Exhibit 6.2. Sample Questions for Board Performance Assessment

- Does the board set its agenda?
- Is board attendance high or declining?
- Have individual directors visited organizational site?
- Is the board appropriately diverse?
- Is there regular trustee training?
- Is there a trustee code of conduct?
- Does the board meet without the CEO?
- Does the CEO position description exist?
- Are regular evaluations of the CEO conducted?

- Are regular evalutions of the board and its committees conducted?
- Does the board meet with relevant stakeholders?
- Does the board monitor key investments and programs for mission alignment and financial performance?
- Does the board do a 360-degree survey of both itself and the CEO?

Board Formal External Reporting

By U.S. law the nonprofit is a tax-free organization and is exempt from federal and state income taxes. In order to ensure that the organization is compliant, an IRS Form 990 must be filed. Church and certain church-related organizations are exempt from this requirement. The reporting includes

1. Detailed financial information on assets, liabilities, revenues, and expenses for last two years
2. Detailed compensation information
3. Your governance procedures, including its independent election process, and so forth
4. Detailed statement of organization mission
5. Various special requirements for schools, hospitals, and less onerous reporting for nonprofits with gross receipts under $200,000 and assets under $500,000

By U.S. law, the 990 must be reviewed and approved by the board. As a potential new board member you should ask to see it as it provides critical insight into the organization. In the past much of this information such as compensation and expense reimbursement policies were tightly held information by a subset of the executive committee.

Summary

These issues of building, structuring, and evolving the board are very sensitive and very critical. This is why the selection of the head of the governance committee is important. A tactful person with a deep sense of the organization's mission and history, and strong links to the various constituencies affected by the organization, is critical. This is not a job for a junior trustee.

Questions the Trustee Should Ask

Appropriate board structure and processes are essential for the nonprofit. Key questions the trustee must ask include:

- Is the organization's governance committee executing a strategic view? Is the organization developing a new generation of leaders?
- Are the various finance committees staffed and structured to execute the board's fiduciary responsibilities?
- Is the development committee appropriately staffed for its long-term contribution?
- Is the plant appropriately maintained?
- Have all board members internalized the mission? Is renewal of internalization a regular process?
- Is the executive committee playing a constructive role?
- Are board and committee meetings designed to bring out the best in the trustees?

7

LEADERSHIP CHAIRMAN AND CEO–A COMPLEX PARTNERSHIP

At the heart of a nonprofit's performance is an effective leadership team. The role and nature of leadership is a deeply interesting and complex topic that has been the subject of endless research and scholarly writing in recent years. We do not plan to enter that debate in this book but rather focus on what is special about nonprofit leadership. There are several distinguishing aspects to consider.

1. The clear duality of the role of the paid CEO of the organization and that of the unpaid chairman of the board, to whom ultimate responsibility devolves. The nonexecutive chair, a widely used organizational concept in the United Kingdom corporate sphere (although the chairman is paid), has only recently emerged in the U.S. corporate world— again with a paid chairman.

2. Performing and growing in a world of ambiguous performance measures. For all its flaws, measuring performance against budgeted earnings, ROI targets, and growth targets both clarifies the task of leadership in the for-profit world and how one approaches its evaluation. Assessing performance against mission and its sustainability is the harder and more complex task faced in the nonprofit world. In Chapter Three we focused on the issues involved in developing and using these measures. The reality, however, is they are not

as crisp and are more subject to interpretation than for-profit measures. The ability to understand, articulate, and lead mission evolution is consequently at the heart of nonprofit leadership. The leaders who do not deeply believe in and have the ability to communicate the mission of their organizations have a real problem.

3. The direct and personal role that the nonprofit leaders must take in fund-raising activities. As noted in Chapter Five, the chairman of the board and the CEO are both deeply and continuously involved in this activity. This is not an episodic event like raising money for a venture capital fund but rather is an ongoing part of the leaders' task.

The board's most important tasks regarding CEO leadership are selecting the leader (and selling the individual on the job), introducing the individual to the organization, coaching the individual during his or her career, and of course, evaluation of performance. Of course, none of this is a science, but rather an art. The consequences, however, of getting it right or wrong can be extraordinary. Two contrasting real-world examples follow.

Several decades ago, a school in the midst of emerging financial turmoil and some staff alienation conducted a CEO search. The candidate ultimately selected was young, charismatic, and a great teacher. The candidate also had zero administrative experience and had never spent an hour in an educational institution of this form. Within three months, this new CEO's early staffing and educational policy decisions, quickly implemented and not thought through, triggered a staff union election that was barely beaten back four months later. In the turmoil of the aftermath, the school sought a new CEO who was mature and had previous experience in dealing with these kinds of issues. Even so, her initial introduction was very rough and, indeed, twenty years later when the authors visited the school, there were still echoes and memories of this incident and the resulting decade of unrest.

Exactly the opposite took place at Mt. Auburn Hospital.[1] In 1998, this midsize community health care hospital was facing significant losses and a polarized, unhappy physician community. To the surprise of all, into this environment a nurse administrator who came from a much smaller hospital was selected as CEO. The results were extraordinary. Indeed, a decade later, the hospital would rank as one of the most profitable, high-quality institutions in its region, and it had a remarkably enthusiastic and supportive physician community, the majority of whom were major contributors to the annual fund. At the center of this transformation was an energetic, deeply empathetic individual with physician and nursing quality care issues. She was able to build a new staff, launch and culminate a successful capital campaign for new facility construction in 2008, and drive the hospital's quality of care indices sharply upwards. An organization that could have gone under instead went the other way.

It is the authors' contention that leaders do make a difference and that the most important task of a board is to get these decisions right. The single most important ad hoc committee of the board is the CEO search committee, as will be described. Get it right and the framework for success is set. Get it wrong, as Harvard did with Larry Summers, and you can deal the organization real short-term harm, as well as potential long-term damage.

Looking at the other side of the leadership duo, the chairman is also critical and is indeed more important than is seen at first blush. When everything is on course in the organization, the role of the chairman is significant. She presides over board meetings, works closely with all the key committee chairs, and is in constant contact with the CEO on both operational and strategic issues. The chair must be close to the CEO but not too close (in a well-studied HBS case, the class almost unanimously concludes that keeping a pair of running shoes of the CEO in the chair's New York apartment was a bit over the top).

The reality of the job, however, is more complicated. Not only must the chair provide regular input to the CEO on her performance, but in the case of a crisis (death, resignation, or dismissal of the CEO) ultimate management responsibility for the organization may pass to the chair. She may act as interim CEO, or appoint an interim CEO while the board launches and staffs a search committee.

Unfortunately, these are mostly unplanned events. Consequently, the chair must be a person of credibility to the rest of the board, possess good judgment, and deeply understand the mission of the organization—so that he or she will have the necessary autonomy to take necessary steps. In no case was this more clear than when Alfred Koppel, an alum, long-term trustee, and the chairman of Trinity College, Connecticut, was dealing with the departure of his CEO to a prestigious archrival in the mid-1990s.[2] Alfred, although angry and embarrassed by the event, publicly handled the transition with great grace. In talking about his handling of it with one of the coauthors, Alfred noted that at its core, Trinity was an educational institution. In his judgment, how this highly emotional and visible event was handled would send an important message to students about what values and style of behavior the institution stood for and what it expected in its alumni. Appropriate, swift action with dignity, not a vitriolic scorched-earth policy was the message he wanted to deliver. It was, in short, a mission-relevant teachable moment that was seized by the chairman. A sister institution under similar circumstances acted quite differently.

CEO Search

We will not deal with the special issues of start-up CEOs in this chapter. As noted earlier, we believe that the search for a CEO is the single most important task of a board. Done well, it sets the context for success. Done poorly, it can paralyze the organization. The search begins with the selection of an appropriate search committee composed of trustees who have a broad view of the institution's future and its position in the community and industry, and who deeply understand its mission. For institutions that have "professionals" such as hospitals, universities, and schools, representatives of these constituencies are normally also represented on the committee. Because of the confidentiality of these deliberations, these individuals find themselves often partially estranged from their communities as they cannot share the specific contents of the meetings, a condition that needs to be clearly recognized at the outset. All committee members must understand the time commitments of this task and be able to make it work in their personal schedules. Committee meetings, candidate interviews, reviewing CVs, and consultant selections all take time, and almost everyone needs to be there for those activities.

Unless there is an overwhelmingly dominant internal candidate, prevailing practice is to retain a consultant whose job is to broaden the pool of candidates and to help manage candidate relationships as they move through the process, so that people don't drop out through misunderstandings. The consultant plays a key role in helping both sides come together. Even in the case of a strong internal candidate, an external search process is often justified as a way of legitimizing the internal candidate in the eyes of the community. All of this can easily consume six or more months under optimal conditions.

There are, of course, exceptions to the rule. The authors remember a case where the combination of a strong internal candidate, a financially precarious situation of the organization, a history of failed external hires, and the support of the previous CEO caused the board not to do an external search. In this situation, the board's decision that a bird in the hand was worth two in the bush turned out to be correct, launching a very successful fourteen-year CEO career. The reality is that it is hard to make administrative generalizations about ideal search processes as there are so many extenuating circumstances.

When the search committee initially convenes, its first task is to get to know each other and establish working relationships. Although the trustees on the committee may know each other, they may not know many of the professionals, and vice versa. This process overlaps with the committee's most important early task, namely identifying the requirements for the "candidate." It is very important to have the consultants there, to size up who says what, the passion and thought behind comments, and, equally important, what was not said. This refining of job specifications is likely to continue for several meetings. Indeed, to some extent this will persist through the candidate interviews, as seeing and listening to actual candidates sharpens thoughts as to what the board is looking for (and what they are not).

These discussions can be intense and lengthy. The heat comes from the fact that though the mission may not be in question, exactly where the organization is in its execution and what are likely to be the organization's short- and medium-term challenges are topics that need to be hammered out and a consensus reached. Some representative quotes from recent search committees capture the full range of issues:

- "We need a youngish CEO. Our most significant leaders were here over twenty years."
- "We need someone with strong interpersonal skills to mend a fractured organization. Vision and strategy are in pretty good shape."
- "Need someone with a strong focus on internal issues. Improved quality is our number one challenge."
- "Must have strong fund-raising skills. Our lack of success under the predecessor in this area has left us vulnerable."
- "Need to raise intellectual productivity standards of faculty. We are losing ground in this area."

If possible it is useful to have the incoming (or continuing) chairman be on the committee. This helps ensure a good relationship between the chair and the new CEO from the begin-ning. It cannot be emphasized enough that getting the right per-son must dominate the desirability of getting the search done on time. If you slip on the recruiting schedule, you can always retain some form of interim leader to help you limp through. If you get it wrong, undoing and restarting a search process can be in-credibly painful and time-consuming. The process of correcting a false start can cause years of work on programs to be postponed.

Arrival of the CEO

The early months of the CEO's presence, as in the for-profit world, are critical in helping to ensure success. The search com-mittee's final task before disbanding is to help organize the wel-coming and orientation activities. Very quickly, however, the power and the ability to manage the agenda for the organization's operations falls to the CEO. Some critical observations are:

- Relatively speaking, the first year is a honeymoon period. There is a feeling of excitement and energy and a new programmatic focus. It is an ideal time to launch significant initiatives. The challenge, however, is that at the beginning you don't know enough to be sure footed in identifying and making the appropriate changes. Conversely, as time passes the more comfortable you will become in what you are doing, but the harder it is to get major change done as internal resistance builds.

- Pace of change is heavily dictated by what you walk into. On one extreme was the person walking into an organization which had been headed by the same individual for over twenty-five years and who was widely seen to be an industry icon. The new CEO mostly spent the first year observing and learning. In so doing she began to see the strain lines and stresses behind the façade. She then carefully used staff and a trustee committee plus a new COO to pick up these issues and begin to generate discussion and action steps. A decade later, she is still talked about as the industry exemplar of taking over a successful organization and appropriately transforming it. Her new initiatives left the organization's programs fully modernized and its finances in great shape. The first five years' initiatives were largely programmatic and related to staff reconstruction. The last five were focused on building and capital fund-raising, not an unusual sequence. All of this was possible because of the good initial work done by the search committee.

At the other extreme was a new CEO taking over a financially challenged organization which many observers felt was about to fail. Several months before he took charge, a consulting report had been delivered to the organization describing what it had to do to succeed, and the task was feasible in the consultant's judgment. The report concluded, however, by noting that in the author's professional judgment the organization's troubled internal culture would prevent them from undertaking these steps and predicted that they would be bankrupt and out of business in six months. The new CEO saw no need to keep this pain to himself. He posted the entire report, including all recommendations, on the organization's Web site so that every employee from the lowest-level janitor to the highest-ranked professional could clearly see that a dispassionate professional organization had classified them as a group of incompetent losers who would fail through their own ineptitude. This immediate slap in the face by the outsider set the stage for the acceptance of an aggressive series of cost cutting and hiring and firing decisions by the new CEO that almost immediately started to right the ship. Within two years the organization had been returned to profitability. In this case, the action had to be immediate.

Balance. The incoming CEO needs to balance strategic change with the turmoil, hostility, and so forth that can come from such a move, as each change tends to gore the ox of some internal constituency. Each change can slowly erode support, even if it turns out to be ultimately successful programmatically. One of the most effective transformational nonprofit CEOs we know implemented two dramatic organization-changing programs. The first involved the escalation of a not very popular program which the CEO felt was critical to balance the long-term service profile of the organization to different constituencies. Supported by the board after an all-day retreat, its implementation required heavy investment and curtailing of a popular program, which caused significant dismay among a portion of its serviced constituencies. In retrospect it was a critical organization-saving step. The second program was seen as appropriate modernizing of an existing program and also involved heavy investments (diverting money from other programs). After four years this was also a success. Unfortunately, the CEO then tried to implement a third program in what was by then a stressed organization. The third move involved elimination of staff and programs particularly dear to a very real constituency. Too much change in too short a time on what was not a life-or-death issue! The organization revolted and the CEO lost his job. Early success blinded his eyes to the intrinsically more complicated third situation. The warning signs were there but he chose not see them.

Other things that are important in helping the newly appointed CEO be successful in the long term include the following:

- *360° annual feedback.* Without this absolutely vital feedback on his performance, the CEO may be losing control and no one, including the CEO, will knows it until it's too late. If the CEO appears not to want feedback she will often be denied it until it is too late. This gap is particularly important in the absence of reliable performance metrics. The surge in adrenaline that comes from doubling sales and return on investment in the for-profit world is not possible here. Intense focus on developing appropriate metrics can somewhat soften this point. Increase in quality results, success in recruiting high profile people, and increases in major gifts are all examples of good indirect surrogate measures of performance. This was discussed at length in Chapter Three.

- *Understand complexity.* The CEO must assess the complexity and measurability of what he is trying to accomplish before he does it. A newly hired college president was brought in by the board to improve the quality of faculty academic outputs. He made the mistake of sharing this goal with the faculty. Furious about his having agreed to this agenda at the time of his hiring, within six months he was chased from office. His successor was more subtle in approaching this agenda.

- *CEO's strength.* It is important to recognize that the CEO is often hired for one set of strengths. Over time his success in dealing with his initial challenges is such that these problems are blunted. Unfortunately the remaining problems may not be in his zone of competence. To survive, the CEO must be able to recognize the issue, hire new staff, and so on to deal with this.

- *CEO-board-chair relationship.* Finally, the CEO's relationship with the board and its chair is critical. Failure to tend to this appropriately can be life threatening to the CEO's tenure.

Board Chair Search

For a variety of reasons, the selection of the board chair is a task second in importance only to the appointment of the head. It is the responsibility of the governance committee to do this using a variety of inputs as noted below. As part of their task they need to

1. Interview each board member individually to understand their views of candidates, the current challenges facing the organization, and the intensity of these views. Clearly, not

all views are weighed the same, but it is important for the committee to understand where all the rocks are located in the river.

2. Assess whether the individual has the skills for the task at hand. A chair coming in at the launch of a capital campaign needs very different skills from one who must lead an organization through a bone-crushing financial crisis. For example, when an organization was getting ready to plan its first debt offering, the selection of a bank president as board chair brought appropriate perspective to the task and a sense of comfort to all constituencies, particularly because in their eighty-year history they had never had any debt. Another organization, in the midst of a major industry consolidation, felt it would have to merge and consequently picked a chair who had substantial experience in mergers. His first step as chair was to recruit to the board two other members who had skills for planning and implementing mergers.

3. Assess whether the individual has the temperament and breadth for this assignment. As noted earlier, during a period of transition in the case of a sudden CEO resignation or death, all authority may come de facto to the chairman. Consequently it is a great deal more than an honorific title. A deep understanding of the organization's operations and mission is critical for the board chair at that moment

4. Ask if the individual has the confidence of the CEO (and is that important?). If the governance committee (and thus a portion of the board) is unhappy with the direction the institution is going, the selection of a chair who has issues with the CEO may be appropriate. To execute this role, an independent governance committee with a strong backbone is key.

Over time some CEO's have been successful in totally capturing control of the board nominating process. In one memorable situation, the CEO was completing his forty-first year with his eightieth birthday just on the horizon. The average board member had twenty-five years' experience, and more than a decade had passed since the last new member was added (against all governance rules of thumb the organization is still doing very well both programmatically and philanthropically). We believe this is the exception to the rule. The selection of the board chair and indeed board members must be firmly in the province of the governance committee.

The committee needs to be specific on both the length of the chair appointment and how many times it can be renewed. The committee must be sure the individual has the time and energy for the task, and that there are no hidden motivational skeletons in his pursuing the job.

Incoming Board Chair Questions

When you are approached to be a board chair, it is almost impossible not to feel pleased at having received this recognition. Because it has been offered, however, does not mean you should automatically accept it. There are some soul-searching questions you must ask before accepting. Failure to answer these questions honestly at this time can lead to great anguish later. These questions include:

1. Do I care deeply about the organization and its mission? Almost always, the job (if well done) winds up taking a great deal more time and effort than anticipated. Note that the job will not be presented to you in that light. If you care deeply about the organization and its mission this time allocation becomes an investment you are happy to make. If you don't, the job can become an increasingly unwelcome burden.

2. Do I deeply understand the competitive dynamics and technologies of the organization and its industry? If you don't, you may make some very poor choices. Some

organizations, such as large museums, hospitals, and universities, are intrinsically very complex. It takes years to understand the broad issues and trends which are buffeting them. For other organizations, the learning curve on these items may be quite short.

3. Do I know why I was selected? Are those reasons and expectations consistent with my interests and abilities? If you are a visionary, for example, and you have been chosen to give the organization a chance to catch its breath after a turbulent time, this assignment may not be a success (unless, of course, unexpected problems emerge). Similarly, if the organization has heavy financial needs and you do not have great turnaround skills, the capacity to personally give a major gift, or the skills to solicit gifts, this is unlikely to work out.

4. Do I have the time to give to the tasks? If an emergency comes, will I be able to step up and give the time it demands? If not, how will the situation get resolved? Is the timing right for me? In a recent search, the most qualified candidate for board chair disqualified himself on the grounds that there was a 50 percent chance of his receiving a major government appointment. Since the board was about to undertake a CEO search, this could have created the possibility of both jobs becoming simultaneously vacant. The board didn't know about this government appointment as a group, and the individual consequently did the organization an enormous favor in withdrawing from consideration.

5. What is my evaluation of the CEO? Will I enjoy working with her? Can the two of us work together? Are our skills complementary or is there the possibility of dangerous reinforcement of perspectives and consequent blind spots? How are the two of us going to interact with each other? Is the CEO going to be comfortable with the processes I plan to use to get data about her performance?

6. Do I have the capacity and patience to really listen? As a normal board member I can let my attention drift at meetings. As a chair I must be on top of all aspects of the board discussion all the time.

7. Do I have a view of who my successor will be and what (if any) training and assignments he will have to undertake to be ready?

8. Has the board designed a process to give me feedback on how I am doing from the perspective of my fellow board members?

Board-Chair Relationship

Absolutely pivotal to the organization, this relationship can develop in many ways depending on the institution and the specific individuals. The most traditional and easy to understand is the relationship between the new CEO and the board chair at the time the CEO was appointed. This is often a close positive relationship, because the chair, if not actually a member of the search committee, was very close to it and was surely part of the final round of interviews. If this interaction did not go well, it is unlikely that the CEO would have been hired.

Almost immediately following the appointment, the relationship begins to evolve in ways that place increasing power and control in the hands of the CEO. Highly visible to the communities surrounding the institution, the CEO is seen as the center of authority and of all detailed knowledge relating to the organization. In fact, the better the chair does his job, if the organization is going well, the less visible he is to these communities. Furthermore, as a general but not universal rule, the chair tends to turn over more rapidly than the CEO (assuming all is going well). By the time the second chair comes in, the CEO is highly visible as the institution's leader and the chair is very much behind the scenes.

Changing chairs is a challenge that must be addressed by the CEO. His warm relationship with the previous chair and their way of sharing insights and making policy and tactical decisions is suddenly all up for grabs. For example, one of the authors is a morning person. Right after he came in as a board chair, he established that once a week he and the CEO would have a 6:30 AM breakfast meeting lasting an hour and a half. This was painful for the CEO, who was a night person, but it worked. Problems and issues were hammered out. Over the four years, a capital campaign was launched and completed, a building constructed, and staff salaries jumped 40 percent. When the board chair stepped down, the CEO stopped the 6:30 AM meetings and a very new set of processes had to be created to deal with the new chair.

What are some of the potential problems in the chair/CEO relationship?

Lack of CEO Accountability. Over time, as chairs rotate, more and more power often accrues to the CEO, who may then become increasingly detached from normal supervision of and accountability to the board. Often accentuated by lack of 360° reviews, the risk exists of increasing alienation between the CEO and the board—until a critical incident occurs and the whole thing blows up. It is the governance committee's job to put appropriate controls in place. This is done most easily at the beginning of a CEO's tenure, when it will seem simply normal practice as far as he is concerned. The problem here is subtle. As long as the imperial CEO is seen as doing a good job objectively, evidenced by improved service levels and good cash flows, the board and the chair can be lulled into complacency. When a crisis emerges, they may neither be trained for nor have the habits for a good response. The aftermath can be ugly.

Chair Seen as CEO's Pet. Minus the normal standards and processes of review of CEO performance, the CEO may influence the governance committee to nominate someone he can safely dominate. Particularly in the absence of executive sessions of the board, this can get out of control. When both the CEO and board chair are tied together in this way, it may be very hard for a normal board member or indeed the whole board to effectively call for improved accountability. Sometimes resignation from the board is the only way to make one's point and one should not hesitate to do it. Over time these pressures tend to accrue.

Close but Not Too Close. The delicacy of the relationship is such that, on the one hand, the chair and CEO need to have a close collaboration regarding strategy and operational issues. On the other hand, there needs to be enough distance so that the chair can make the call that if in his judgment things are not going well, he can provide constructive feedback to the CEO, and if that doesn't work, even harsher remedies. This is unfortunately much easier said than done. One of the board chairs of a leading medical institution told the coauthors that the hardest thing he ever had to do was to fire the CEO who for twenty years had mentored him in so many ways. That it had to be done for the survival of the institution in no way reduced the pain.

Lack of Understanding of Each Other's Weaknesses. One of the situations studied was a board chair who had faced a difficult conundrum. He had a CEO who was doing just OK running the institution. Fragile under interpersonal attacks, the CEO had built up a reservoir of ill will among a fraction of the communities being served by the nonprofit. Though not fatally disabling to the CEO's effectiveness, it was clearly a problem. Coaching over an extended period had not produced results and a transition was in order. At the same time, however, the chairman was ready to start a capital campaign to build a critical new facility that would substantially change the perceived quality of the institution and its service. It was not feasible to do the CEO transition and build the facility simultaneously. After a lot of thought, the chairman decided he could use his personality to cover for the CEO's weakness, and went ahead with the facility. Two years later the facility was built, happily inaugurated, and the chair retired. The following year the pent-up pressures that the chair had held back burst and the CEO was replaced. (Note that the end of a capital campaign is always a dangerous time as pent-up pressures suppressed in the name of the now completed project can suddenly brim over. This needs to be carefully planned for by CEOs who may naively be planning a celebration.) Several years later, the retired chair, while still feeling modestly guilty about the CEO, allowed that if he had to do it all over he would do the same thing. The tradeoff was that the organization had to weather two semi-uneven years of operating performance, in return for a facility that dramatically transformed services far into the future.

Remember the CEO Really Knows Staff. When something is not going well, it is important to remember that by virtue of day-to-day contact, the CEO often has important insight into staff skills that neither the board members nor chair may have. It consequently behooves the chair to listen carefully when the CEO expresses an opinion at variance from his thinking concerning an individual's or program's performance. The authors recall an incident when the board chair expressed concern about the organization's head of development and whether perhaps it was time to make a change, as the development activity was underresourced and going nowhere. The new CEO who had been in place for four months pushed back strongly, saying the existing development head had shaped her role and that of her department to deal with the nondevelopment orientation of the previous CEO. In the new head's judgment, under her leadership the development director would be able to build a staff with the capability to perform at a high level. Two years later, it was apparent to all that this was a correct judgment as the development activities had soared. On other occasions, however, a gentle nudge from the chair has been the impetus for the CEO to deal with something that he knew he really should do, but which for a variety of reasons had not gotten around to doing.

Do Your Strengths and Weaknesses Complement Each Other? This is a very complex sensitive multifaceted question where the answers depend on context and legitimately change over time. Four very different situations capture this complaint.

A Hospital Turnaround. A major institution on the brink of failure picked a gifted turnaround leader from outside the medical field. The chair was supportive but the CEO almost single-handedly over a two-year period arrested the decline by a combination of charisma, strong staff selections, phasing out some programs, and launching new ones. Fully informed, the chair's role was to keep the board in line and offer unmitigated support. The successor to the chair was picked to lead a new capital campaign to stabilize the balance sheet. Both chairs had warm relationships with the CEO, but the CEO did the job that the governance committee hoped for, and was the dominant person.

A School's Growth. Working hand in glove over a several-year period, an experienced board chair and a new CEO executed a complex planning process for a financially struggling nonprofit's future. Eventually a sharply different strategy emerged (which the board bought in to) than had existed before. This led to the need to secure financial resources through a combination of debt and a capital campaign. At every step the chair and the CEO were coequal partners in this effort that contributed heavily to the organization's success.

A Failed Merger. A merger of two similar organizations was approved by the two boards. The CEO of one became the CEO of the merged entity and was charged with executing the merger. The chair of the merged organization, despite considerable for-profit merger experience, did not become engaged in understanding and influencing the merger's operational details but left these to the CEO. What was a supposed merger of equals turned into a complete takeover by one, with every senior staff of the other organization ultimately leaving. The financial results were so appalling at the end of two years that the chair and his executive committee recognized the situation was unviable. After a lot of futile coaching, they concluded that the CEO had to be replaced. A search committee was formed and six months later, the new CEO was in place; in hindsight, this change turned out to be the beginning of a long recovery process. This was a case of an excessively inactive board chair (and board).

An Ambitious Expansion. A new CEO is brought in to energize a staid institution that had been drifting for some time. Several years into the first set of changes, which, though highly beneficial, had caused turmoil in some constituencies, a new board chair was appointed. Enthusiastic about the new changes, he put his full weight behind them and encouraged active exploration of future changes, brooking no dissenting opinions. In the press of the examination of these alternatives, direct links between the board, the organization's staff, and key service constituencies, which had never been too strong, were lost. The ensuing uproar made it ultimately impossible for either the CEO or the chair to stay. New leadership with a more collaborative focus emerged. Ironically, with the passage of time, it became clear that the right strategic moves were made but that the flaw lay in the inability to see and manage the processes of change. Both the chair and CEO were remarkable people but their shared focus on the substance of change rather than the processes of change was their undoing. Either one alone would have been fine, but would have needed a different collaborator to be successful.

Normal Evolution

Over time, of course, individuals change. Normal processes of aging, arrival of some forms of substance abuse, midlife crises, burnout, and so on all mean that the CEOs who are effective leaders at one point in time may have trouble at another point. This requires continual monitoring by the governance committee and board chair. The challenge for the governance committee is to remain close enough to the action through 360° reviews to spot when this is beginning to occur. This is particularly hard for national boards that only meet a few times per year, and whose members are far from the organization's physical center. In this environment we pose a series of questions that both the CEO and the board chair should ask themselves in Exhibits 7.1 and 7.2.

Exhibit 7.1. Questions the CEO Must Periodically Ask Herself

1. Am I still the right person for the job or have I or the organization changed so that there is no longer a good fit? Alternatively, do I need to make changes in staff or structure to deal with the new environment? In the authors' judgment the art of leaving and doing it gracefully is at least as important as the art of entering an organization. Hallmarks of a great CEO are: (1) the ability to help transition key relationships to a successor; (2) leaving some quick wins for her to have as she is learning the ropes; (3) resolving as many messy situations as possible before departing. In the face of a weak board things can become incredibly drawn out. The longest of these processes of which the authors are aware was the nineteenth-century headship of Eliphalet Nott of Union College, a sixty-two-year term which ended in the college's near bankruptcy.

2. Do I still have board support for myself and my programs? Annual counseling sessions with the board chair around the time of compensation determination are very important, particularly if the board is organized well enough to give well-researched substantive inputs to the chair for this session.

---

3. Am I seen as a liability to the organization? How do I know this?

4. Do I have a positive working relationship with the chair? One test of this is whether you feel comfortable having a discussion with him on the topics in this list.

Exhibit 7.2. The Series of Questions That the Board Chair Must Periodically Ask Herself

1. Am I appropriately invisible to the organization? Except in times of crisis, the CEO should almost always be the visible voice of the organization. Publicity about a chair normally occurs when things are not going well.

2. Do I still have the confidence of the board? This is where an annual survey of board members regarding the chair's performance by the governance committee can be very helpful. The combination of the addition of new board members and changing organization challenges make this topic important to visit on a periodic basis. If, for example, the main issues confronting the organization have to do with financial control and you are primarily a growth person, there is a significant mismatch. In an earlier time you may have produced good leadership, but your skills may not fit the new world.

3. Am I aware of new trends in service in my industry and how my organization is positioned against them? Am I satisfied as to how my organization's administrative team is dealing with these challenges?

4. Am I comfortable with my insight as to what is going on inside the organization?

5. Have I identified my successor(s) and are they being put through appropriate development activities?

Summary

This chapter has dealt with some of the most important and complex challenges that the nonprofit board faces. With an effectively functioning leadership team at the top, many things are possible. When inappropriate leaders and communication exist at the top, the organization faces a real burden. In the end sorting these issues out is more of an art than a science. There are not right leaders and communications processes in general. There are, however, right processes and leaders for an organization at a particular point in time. The duality of leadership in the nonprofit makes these issues particularly complex because many board members with a for-profit background do not have experience in dealing with duality.

It should be noted that the best leaders are not necessarily the organization's best teachers, curators, doctors, and so on. They are those who are best able to facilitate the evolution of a long-term vision or strategy and can then mobilize resources to make the strategy happen. These tasks often take a long time to play out, especially in a world where CEOs are spending shorter amounts of time in them before moving on. It has often been noted, for example, that many of the most successful university presidents had terms of twenty years or longer. The combination of tenure and ingrained cultures make these organizations particularly challenging to turn around.

Questions the Trustee Should Ask

The most delicate and important relationship in a nonprofit is that between the chairman and the CEO. Key questions for the trustee:

- Does the organization regularly evaluate the performance of the CEO? Does it give structured feedback to the CEO?

- Do the skills of the chair and the CEO complement each other? Do they work well together?
- Is the CEO search committee (when needed) appropriately staffed? Is the board appropriately involved in the search process?
- Does the CEO regularly ask the questions in Exhibit 7.1?
- Does the chair regularly ask the questions in Exhibit 7.2?
- Does the organization have appropriate backup and transition plans for each job?

8

YOU AS A TRUSTEE

In the context of all the detailed background of the previous chapters, this chapter focuses on a single simple question: what does all this mean to me as a trustee and what should I do? The chapter is divided into five sections.

- Should I accept the invitation to join this nonprofit board or seek another board?
- What should I do before my first meeting?
- What are the key things to do in my first two years on the board?
- What should I do to effectively manage my career as a trustee? How should the role unfold?
- How should I gracefully go about transitioning off the board and into another relationship?

Should I Join the Board?

As one approaches handling the invitation to join a board, a number of questions spring to mind:

1. Do I believe in the mission of the organization as I understand it at this time? Are there aspects that could potentially trouble me and have I really thought them through carefully? For example, as a Catholic on the board

of a secular hospital, am I comfortable about their approach to end-of -life issues?

2. Do I have the time available for this work and does the board calendar work for me? For example, if you have a busy daily work schedule, a board with noontime, midweek meetings will not work.

3. Are there potential conflicts of interest between this organization's board and other activities and have you reviewed these issues with the governance committee?

4. Is the group of trustees a group I would be happy to be associated with in terms of my reputation? Are there downsides? Are these individuals who I would like to know better beyond the context of the nonprofit? Do they help me with my business and allow me to more closely integrate with the community (an ignoble but practical question)?

5. Do I understand what personal financial expectations there are for me and am I comfortable with them? Do I understand what fund-raising is expected of me, and is this something I am comfortable with?

6. Do I have background and skills that are appropriate to the needs of the organization? Will I find this work complementary to the rest of my life?

7. Do I understand what the real reasons are that I have been asked to join the board? Are they appropriate and realistic? If the organization assumes particular skills or financial capabilities you don't have, the relationship will become very awkward.

8. Will my spouse be supportive of this relationship or will it be intrusive? Someone recently asked to be chair of a board tentatively broached the topic to his spouse and was astonished. She stated her strong support in no uncertain terms, noting their family had benefited enormously from the organization, and that he had skills peculiarly

appropriate to their needs. His time away from home would be well spent.

9. Does being a trustee in the organization allow me to pay back an important debt for services the organization gave me? For example, a significant number of hospital trustees are grateful patients, many university trustees are graduates of the school, and so forth.

10. Young trustees are often particularly anxious to join their first board and take the opportunity to contribute to society in this way, and so they will be less demanding in their investigation. Conversely, one particularly experienced nonprofit trustee recently told one of the coauthors that he had reached a stage in his life where he would not consider a board unless there was a reasonable possibility of his being elected chair within a year. In the authors' opinion he had a service record to justify this view.

11. Am I comfortable with the pace of discussion and its content? How do I feel about the organization's leadership team and will I be able to enthusiastically work with them?

12. Have I attended a board meeting to get a feel of what I am getting into? Am I comfortable with the pace of discussion and its content?

13. Have I reviewed the organization's IRS Form 990 and do I understand the mission, governance, and finances of the organization?

In short, there are a number of questions to address before you agree to join a board. Because your reputation and the organization's reputation will become intertwined over time, it is particularly important to be diligent in advance. Of course, in some cases, you may have deliberately sought out the opportunity for personal reasons. In these cases, absent some startling revelation, it is easy to make the decision. Many of the above questions are easy to answer whereas others may be complicated.

How Do I Get Started?

How do I get prepared? Unless this is a brand-new nonprofit, you are coming into an organization with a history and culture that you probably do not understand, or even worse, think you do understand (but in reality don't). Following is one of the great HBS cases on this topic, "Harold Morton and the Rivendell Board."[1]

Harold Morton and the Rivendell Board

Harold Morton, who had graduated ten years earlier from Rivendell, was driving to his first trustees' meeting. Harold was excited because it was his first visit back to the campus since graduation and the key item on his first meeting's agenda was selecting between two finalists the new president of Rivendell. Harold's preparation for the meeting was a fifteen-minute board orientation he had had with the board chair, of which half the time was spent talking about the chairman's daughter, a classmate of Harold's. He had also read the two finalists' detailed resumés. Harold, as he told one of the coauthors, was genuinely excited in advance about the contribution he was going to make to the meeting as someone who had had a happy educational experience there ten years earlier (but absolutely no other contact).

Arriving just on time for the meeting, the only vacant chair in the room was the one next to the previous chair of the board, so Harold took it. A half hour into the meeting, Harold leaned forward to make his first comments as a board member. As he opened his mouth to talk, he felt the previous chair's hand on his right shoulder, pulling him back into his seat. Surprised and shocked, he said nothing. Twice more in the next hour, the same thing happened and Harold finally stepped back and listened. Discussing it nearly a decade later, when Harold was about to become board chair, he reflected that the former board chair's intervention was extremely fortunate. Harold noted that when he joined, he did not know what he didn't know. Had he jumped into the conversation demonstrating no awareness of the administrative complexities of the college on the basis of his ten-year-old experience as a student, he would have looked shallow. Not only did he have no insight on the institution's finances, faculty morale, adequacy of endowment current strategy, and so forth, but as a brand-new trustee he had not participated in the nearly nine-month-long dialogue on the issues that had shaped the search and led to these final two candidates. Harold clearly drew the contrast in his mind between heavyweight and lightweight trustees, and how important it is to get off on the right foot if you are to be seen as a heavyweight trustee. A narrow, insensitive focus presented in your first couple of comments to the whole board can paint you into a corner relating to your perceived competence, from which it may be impossible to escape in the next five years.

Interestingly, when the coauthors teach the case, the class (whether MBAs or experienced executives) tends to split right down the middle on this issue. Half the class says that Harold has a viewpoint that the other board members should hear. They also note that it is likely that this will be his only chance to talk about a CEO search as, when the next one comes around ten years later, he most likely will have served his term and be off the board. The other half of the class vehemently disagree, saying it is better to keep your mouth shut and let people think you are stupid than open it and confirm their belief. After the discussion is concluded and we show them an eight-minute video of Harold talking about this, almost unanimously the group concludes in this case that silence is the better part of wisdom. At the core of this example is the notion that the longer you serves as a trustee, the more valuable you become as you gain context. There is a necessary familiarization and maturation process with an organization that is very hard to accelerate.

Once you have made the decision to join the board, there are a number of things you need to do to get ready for your first meeting. Some of these you will have already done in preparation for your decision to join the board but are also mentioned here for the sake of completeness.

1. Get the dates and times for the meetings for the next two years and resolve as many conflicts as possible. Try to organize your schedule to be at the meeting at least a half hour early and to not be rushed at meeting's end. This informal networking time is very useful in both getting to know staff and other board members, their names, personalities, interests, their issues, and their backgrounds. Often as much is learned and done at these times as in the formal board meeting. The trustee who rushes in late and leaves right at the end misses important occasions to gain context.

2. Attend an orientation session for new board members. If none is planned, do a site visit and meet individually with the CEO and her direct reports. If possible, observe how service is being delivered. You will quickly form opinions on morale, age of premises, types of clientele, and the like that you cannot get from reports or talking only with the CEO. One of the hallmarks of a healthy board and organization is that they encourage you to make this visit and have those one-on-one discussions.

3. Read carefully the current financial statements, including the budget, and audit reports to understand fully what the financial health of the organization that you are walking into. Sometimes a meeting with the CFO to clarify these issues is very helpful.

4. Meet with the chair of the board. This is an important opportunity to discuss your initial committee assignments. Your initial committee assignments are particularly important in gaining insight into the key issues facing the organization and getting to know board and staff better. This is particularly critical because so much of most board's business is done in committee.

5. If you have not done so, surface any conflicts of interest and review them carefully with the CEO. In practical terms, this may mean not voting on certain items, or absenting yourself from either board or committee meetings when certain topics are discussed. Of course, there are occasionally times when the conflict of interest is so clear that it is best not to join the board.

6. Study the bios of your other board colleagues to gain insight into their interests and to facilitate your informal conversations. The really well-organized board will have a board book with this information complete with pictures (some organizations may present this information on a Web site).

7. Make sure you understand any outstanding lawsuits and their status. Satisfy yourself that appropriate trustee liability insurance is in place, and if appropriate legal counsel has been retained. This is an unfortunate reality of twenty-first-century life.

8. Begin listening to perceptions of your organizations' services in the various communities it impacts. In a real way, on the one hand you have become part of the organization's eyes and ears and on the other hand, an ambassador.

9. Be as strategic as possible in asking for your committee assignments. Early in your career, you want to be on a committee that is close to mission in action to really gain insight to the organization's values and services. Soon

enough, you will wind up on the finance committee and development committee. You will be much more effective in these roles as a result of the early insights you have gained on the organization's mission and the people who are executing it.

10. Work to learn the names and interests of the key staff and fellow board members. Doing so dramatically increases your personal effectiveness. We strongly encourage wearing name tags on the right of your jacket (not the left) and having big name cards in front of board members to help jog name recollection. This is particularly important for national boards that only meet three or four times a year.

The reality is that many of these ideas are common sense but the authors are impressed by how many "lightweight" trustees ignore them and find themselves categorized in a way they are uncomfortable with, and which ultimately affects both the quality of their board service and how they feel about it.

First Two Years on the Board

For many organizations, particularly the large and complex ones, the first two years have a large learning component with them. This learning concerns industry context and what is possible to fix in the short run. What can be fixed in the long run, what are the sacred cows, and where is change almost impossible? An example of this challenge is Harvard's decentralized "Every tub on its own bottom" organizational structure; despite forty years of board and CEO work to change it, things remain remarkably constant in this area.

In your first two years, particularly important items are the following:

1. Work to gain insight into the mission, the technology of the organization, and the barriers to the organization

moving forward. For an organization like a homeless shelter, this may be relatively easy to grasp. For a large teaching hospital it takes years to master the winds of public policy debate, the intricacies of reimbursement mechanisms, and the opportunities or challenges posed by new radiology and pharmacological treatments. Membership on the right task forces and committees can accelerate one's learning. A particularly effective one on which one of the coauthors served was a hospital's medical affairs committee, which discussed all the adverse outcomes and potential malpractice cases. Two years of debate as to what quality was and how to measure it made a profound impact in the author's insight into what a well-functioning hospital was all about.

2. Make a real effort to get to know your fellow board members and their perspectives. Coffee breaks, meals, receptions, and so on are all good places to advance your understanding of their perspective.

3. Keep your early comments in meetings succinct until you have enough background to know what you are talking about. People will remember your first couple of comments, and if these seem superficial or wide of the mark, will use them to classify you in ways that are not an accurate representation of your skills.

4. Work to keep your meeting attendance high for the first six months as you establish your overt commitment to the organization in the eyes of both staff and fellow board members.

5. If available and you can squeeze in the time, attendance at an industry seminar for directors can be very helpful. This will give you context for how issues are playing out beyond your organization, and will give you a network of people who are facing similar challenges and to whom you can turn for advice in difficult situations.

6. In the second year try to join a committee that is beyond your comfort zone as you broaden yourself beyond the "functional specialist" role. At the same time, if you have deep financial skills it is time for you to join one of the finance-oriented committees.

7. Work to sharpen your understanding of when the combination of your skills and interests will enable you to make your contribution to the organization over the term(s) of your service. You will want to review this with both the chair and head of the governance committee.

8. Continue to pledge at an appropriate level for your organization. As a general rule of thumb we hope trustees will consider organizations whose board they are on to be one of their top two or three philanthropic interests. At the same time, we acknowledge that an organization should not be too reliant on any one source of funding. If there is a falling out with the trustee, this can leave the organization excessively vulnerable. For example, this is a real issue for some churches, where donors don't want to be more than (say) 10 percent of the church's budget. For hierarchical structures like the Episcopal Church, this allows additional fund-raising at the diocesan and national levels (which they are aggressively pursuing) as people diversify their giving to different pockets of the same organization.

Ongoing Board Service

Fully acclimated to the board after two years, your service will potentially evolve in many ways depending on your interests and skills and the nature of the organization's challenges. Some general comments on relevant issues are offered in the subsequent paragraphs.

For the really interested trustee, time commitment can grow until burnout may become a real problem. This is a topic both you and the governance committee need to keep an eye on. If you have just led a capital campaign or chaired a search committee, a less onerous assignment is appropriate for the next several years as you decompress.

The governance committee each year should review each trustee's current roles and consider what future ones they might undertake and when. You need to have a personal discussion with them about this each year.

Over time your interest in the organization may begin to drift. It may be because your life or priorities have changed. Moving your residence, promotions, and family illness are examples of this. You will feel an erosion of your meeting attendance and participation at special events. If the governance committee is skilled there often are tasks that can rejuvenate your enthusiasm, such as chairing a search, chairing a special program for evaluation, chairing one of the advisory boards, and so forth. As a trustee, however, you have to continually ask yourself whether you want to intensify your effort or whether you have basically made your contribution and your interests have moved to other topics. If so, give the board ample warning of this so your position can be filled. We should point out that in many cases it is inappropriate to stay on in hopes of becoming the chair. As noted in Chapter Seven, a variety of complex issues surround this topic and you may simply be the wrong person at the wrong time for the organizations' needs.

Mission may change in such a way that you as a trustee are no longer comfortable with the organization's direction, and feel that as a matter of principle, you must resign. For example, when a previously single-sex college went coed under a variety of financial pressures, it was not surprising that several trustees who did not argue with the decision resigned in protest. Another recent example is the turmoil in the Episcopal Church where parishes have split off and joined the Anglican Communion. These were cases where the evolving interpretation of mission made it impossible for the members of these parishes to go along with the majority of parishes. Though not frequent,

these are soul-searing events that often have adverse consequences for the organization.

Transition

The reality is that in the overwhelming majority of situations, the
time eventually comes for you to step down from the board. Your
nonrenewable term has expired or you are on a one-year renew-
able office appointment which you have elected to let expire, and
so on. As noted in Chapter One, unlike the for-profit world, in
the nonprofit world the nurturing and maintenance of the relationship beyond board service is very important. It may take
place in a number of ways. These are options for the most part
not within your control but ones which the organization needs to
be attentive to. Examples of these include:

1. Your appointment to an advisory committee, a group of
   retired trustees who meet once a year, or as a member of the
   corporation who elects the trustees, and the like. Each
   organization develops its own mechanisms for these types of
   appointments. For the most part, individuals in these roles
   are invaluable sources of insight during the organization's
   difficult transitions, because of their institutional memory
   and philanthropic support. These points of contact are all
   above and beyond the one-way mailings to you of alumni
   bulletins, newsletters, and Web site updates.

2. Assignment as a member of special task forces such as
   program evaluation, CEO position searches, feasibility
   of capital campaign goals, and so forth.

3. Awarding of an honorary degrees, appointment as an
   honorary trustee, recipient of distinguished service awards,
   accompanied by gala celebrations. These are very special
   and memorable honors and occasions which can be done
   for only a very few trustees.

4. You and the governance committee should pay particular attention to your last one to two years of committee assignments. In a real sense they are the pinnacle of your service and should be in areas that are particularly close to your passion and interest in the organization. For example, a particularly good recent appointment was someone who joined the governance committee and then in the last year became its chair. She left feeling she had made a substantive contribution to the organization and three years later is more committed to and supportive of the cause than ever before.

What is critical is that in the search for new donors and trustees it is easy to lose track of friends and former trustees who, if appropriately recognized, could provide continuing support (both financial and other) in so many ways for the rest of their lives. One of the authors recently gave a speech to the sixtieth reunion class of a professional school and was truly touched and startled by the energy and commitment of these mid-eighty-year-olds to the organization. He nearly skipped it as not being worth the time. That would have been a big mistake.

The above paragraphs focus on your departure where there has been mutual satisfaction on both sides. There are, unfortunately, situations where for a variety of reasons, it has not ended well with you either resigning on principle or being pushed off the board. Oddly enough, despite the pain and passion of the moment, over time even these wounds begin to soften and your position may change. Three examples follow:

One of the authors had responsibility for alumni relations in his university. Every year a significant number of prominent alumni's children were turned down. His job was to call these alums, give them the news, listen to them vent, and be as supportive as possible in helping the child in other ways. It was his least favorite activity of the year, but at least two-thirds of the calls were positive in tone, often with the alum specifically thanking him for reaching out and talking. Many ultimately remained committed and financially supportive of the institution in subsequent years. It was an effective damage-containment strategy. Then there is the case of alum who, thirty years after his son was poorly handled by an institution, is still waiting for the CEO to resign before resuming his donor relationship.

In another case, the mission of an autonomous unit of a nonprofit was dramatically changed by the new CEO who, after five years, was able to pack the board with a majority of his supporters. In deep anger, the trustee resigned from the unit's board and nullified his large six-figure pledge. After soul searching, the trustee reached out to another unit of the same organization whose mission had not changed, gave them the six-figure pledge. Ultimately he became responsible for the leadership of the new unit's capital campaign. In this case, having a structure with multiple giving pockets was advantageous.

Finally, there was the trustee who resigned because of highly unfavorable publicity about his outside activities. Throughout the years, the institution never wavered in its support for him as an individual and refused to be drawn into the inflammatory public debate. Some years later, with the public debate over, he quietly gave a building in the name of one of the institution's great professionals.

In short, in some cases memories soften over time and the relationship can be resumed. There are other situations, however, which are simply irretrievable and both sides have to go on.

Summary

At the end we return to where we started this book. At the core nonprofit boards operations are appropriately quite different from those of their for-profit brethren. Beyond all the issues raised in this book, there is one more critical point. Participation on a nonprofit board can be very spiritually and emotionally rewarding. The authors usually return from their for-profit board meetings excited, challenged, and pleased with being able to deliver important value-added products to the world, for which they are appropriately compensated.

At its core, the nonprofit board is not a commercial but a giving relationship. What makes the relationship so special is the free act of giving time, talent, and treasure to in some way improve the human condition. One of the coauthor's happiest memories is as a school chair finishing his 6:30 AM meeting with the head and, as he was leaving, being overwhelmed by five-year-olds crowding into the school (in his mind they are frozen in time as five-year-olds although today they are towering young adults in their mid-twenties). It was a different feeling from beating a hostile takeover or winning a $3 billion contract. Just different. Welcome to this very exciting part of the world. We look forward to hearing your stories.

Questions the Trustee Should Ask

The most fundamental question this book helps answer is: should I join a nonprofit board and how should I behave? At the core these questions can be simplified.

- Do I viscerally believe in the organization's mission? Do I have a passion for it?
- Do I have the time and energy to do what is needed?
- Does this fit with the totality of the business, family, and community activities I am engaged in? Does my family agree?
- Does the organization's calendar of events and meetings match the slots in my schedule? If not, is there flexibility on either side?
- Do I want to be just a supportive board member or an active player? Are those expectations realistic?

Notes

Chapter One: Introduction

1. Putnam, R. D. *Bowling Alone: The Collapse and Revival of American Community*. New York: Simon & Schuster, 2000.
2. McFarlan, F. W., Leonard, H. B., and Tritter, M. "Dana Hall: Funding a Mission (B)." *Harvard Business School* (Case #306–100), 2007.
3. Leonard, H. B., Epstein, M. J., and Winig, L. "Playgrounds and Performance: Results Management at KaBOOM (A)." *Harvard Business School* (Case #306–031), 2005.
4. Adapted from Leonard, Epstein, and Winig, 2005.
5. Adapted from CMA Canada Partnership Strategic Performance Measures (November 2008). Source: Epstein and Rejc Buhovac, 2009.
6. Epstein, M. J., and Rejc Buhovac, A. "Improving Performance Measurement: Not-for-Profit Organizations." *CMA Management*, November 2009, 16–21.

Chapter Two: Mission

1. McFarlan, F. W., and Vitali, M. R. "From Little Things Big Things Grow: The Clontarf Foundation Program for Aboriginal Boys." *Harvard Business School* (Case #910–402), 2009.

Chapter Three: Performance Measurement

1. Epstein, M. J., and Rejc Buhovac, A. "Improving Performance Measurement: Not-for-Profit Organizations." *CMA*

Management, November 2009, 16–21; Epstein, M. J., and Rejc Buhovac, A. "Performance Measurement of Not-for-Profit Organizations." *Society of Management Accountants of Canada* and *American Institute of Certified Public Accountants,* 2009.

2. Leonard, H. B., Epstein, M. J., and Tritter, M. "Opportunity International: Measurement and Mission." *Harvard Business School* (Case #307–067), 2007.

3. Datar, S. M., Leonard, H. B., Epstein M. J., and Goodwin, T. F. "AARP Foundation (A) & (B)." *Harvard Business School* (A—Case #107–051) (B—Case #107–052), 2007.

4. Leonard, Epstein, and Tritter, 2007.

5. Datar, Leonard, Epstein, and Goodwin, 2007.

Chapter Four: Financial Strategy and Oversight

1. McFarlan, F. W., Leonard, H. B., and Tritter, M. "Dana Hall: Funding a Mission (B)." *Harvard Business School* (Case #306–100), 2007.

2. Jonker, K. "In the Black with BRAC." *Stanford Social Innovation Review,* Winter 2009, 7(1): 74–79.

3. Foster, W., and Bradach, J. "Should Nonprofits Seek Profits?" *Harvard Business Review,* February 2005, 83(2): 92–100.

4. Epstein, M. J., and Rejc Buhovac, A. "Performance Measurement of Not-for-Profit Organizations." *Society of Management Accountants of Canada* and *American Institute of Certified Public Accountants,* 2009.

5. Charity Navigator. www.charitynavigator.org. 2006.

6. Kamenetz, A. "When the Giving Gets Tough." *Fast Company,* May 2008, *125:* 65–66.

7. Ethics Resource Center. *Ethics Resource Center's National Government Ethics Survey: An Inside View of Public Sector Ethics.* Arlington, VA: ERC, 2007.

Chapter Five: Philanthropy

1. The Foundation Center. Retrieved May 26, 2010, from http://foundationcenter.org.

Chapter Six: Board Structure and Role

1. Adapted from Epstein, M. J., and Roy, M. J., "Measuring and Improving the Performance of Corporate Boards." *Society of Management Accountants of Canada*, 2002.
2. Ibid.
3. Adapted and abridged from Epstein, M. J., and Roy, M. J., "Strategic Management of Information for Boards." *Society of Management Accountants of Canada, American Institute of Certified Public Accountants* and *Chartered Institute of Management Accountants (UK)*, 2007.

Chapter Seven: Leadership Chairman and CEO-a Complex Partnership

1. Roberts, L. M., and Kanji, A. "Jeanette Clough at Mt. Auburn Hospital." *Harvard Business School* (Case #406–068), 2005.
2. McFarlan, F. W., and Elias, J. "Trinity College (A) (B) & (C)." *Harvard Business School* (A—Case #397–068) (B—Case #397–069) (C—Case #397–070), 1997.

Chapter Eight: You as a Trustee

1. McFarlan, F. W., and Vargas, I. "Harold Morton and the Rivendell Board (A) & (B)." *Harvard Business School* (A—Case #303–114) (B—Case #303–115), 2003.

References and Reading List for Senior Managers and Board Members

Chait, R. P., Ryan, W. P., and Taylor, B. E. *Governance as Leadership: Reframing the Work of Nonprofit Boards*. Hoboken, NJ: Wiley, 2004.

Charity Navigator. www.charitynavigator.org. 2006.

Datar, S. M., Epstein, M. J., and Yuthas, K. "In Microfinance, Clients Must Come First." *Stanford Social Innovation Review*, Winter 2008, 6(1): 38–45.

Datar, S. M., Epstein, M. J., and Yuthas, K. "Enamored with Scale: Scaling with Limited Impact in the Microfinance Industry." In P. N. Bloom and E. Skloot (eds.), *Scaling Social Impact: New Thinking*. London: Palgrave Macmillan, 2010.

Datar, S. M., Epstein, M. J., and Yuthas, K. "Management Accounting and Control: Lessons for and from the World's Tiniest Businesses." *Strategic Finance*, November 2009, 91(5): 27–34.

Epstein, M. J. *Making Sustainability Work: Best Practices in Managing and Measuring Corporate Social, Environmental, and Economic Impacts*. San Francisco: Berrett-Koehler, 2008.

Epstein, M. J., and Rejc Buhovac, A. "Improving Performance Measurement: Not-for-Profit Organizations." *CMA Management*, November 2009, 16–21.

Epstein, M. J., and Rejc Buhovac, A. "Performance Measurement of Not-for-Profit Organizations." *Society of Management Accountants of Canada and American Institute of Certified Public Accountants*, 2009.

Epstein, M. J., and Roy, M. J. "Measuring and Improving the Performance of Corporate Boards." *Society of Management Accountants of Canada*, 2002.

Epstein, M. J., and Roy, M. J. "Strategic Management of Information for Boards." *Society of Management Accountants of Canada and American Institute of Certified Public Accountants*, 2007.

Epstein, M. J., and Yuthas, K. "Mission Impossible: Diffusion and Drift in the Microfinance Industry." *Sustainability Accounting, Management and Policy Journal*, 2011.

Ethics Resource Center. *Ethics Resource Center's National Government Ethics Survey: An Inside View of Public Sector Ethics*. Arlington, VA: ERC, 2007.

Fleishman, J. L. *The Foundation: A Great American Secret*. New York: Joel L. Fleishman, PublicAffairs, 2007.

Foster, W., and Bradach, J. "Should Nonprofits Seek Profits?" *Harvard Business Review*, February 2005, 83(2): 92–100.

Fremont-Smith, M. R. *Governing Nonprofit Organizations: Federal and State Law and Regulation*. Cambridge, MA: Belknap Press, 2004.

Hertzlinger, R. E. "Effective Oversight: A Guide for Nonprofit Directors." *Harvard Business Review*, July-August 1994, 72(4): 52–60.

Jonker, K. "In the Black with BRAC." *Stanford Social Innovation Review*, Winter 2009, 7(1): 74–79.

Kamenetz, A. "When the Giving Gets Tough." *Fast Company*, May 2008, 125: 65–66.

Letts, C. W., Ryan, W. P., and Grossman, A. *High Performance Nonprofit Organizations: Managing Upstream for Greater Impact*. New York: Wiley, 1998.

McFarlan, F. W. "Working on Nonprofit Boards: Don't Assume the Shoe Fits." *Harvard Business Review*, November-December 1999, 77(6): 64–80.

Nanus, B., and Dobbs, S. *Leaders Who Make a Difference*. San Francisco: Jossey-Bass, 1999.

Phills, J. A., Jr. *Integrating Mission and Strategy for Nonprofit Organizations*. New York: Oxford University Press, 2005.

Rangan, V. K. "Lofty Missions, Down-to-Earth Plans." *Harvard Business Review*, March 2004, 82(3): 112–119.

Wei-Skillern, J. C., Austin, J. E., Leonard, H. B., and Stevenson, H. H. *Entrepreneurship in the Social Sector*. Thousand Oaks, CA: Sage, 2007.

W. K. Kellogg Foundation. *Logic Model Development Guide*. Battle Creek, MI: W. K. Kellogg Foundation, 2004.

Case Studies of Interest

Datar, S. M., Leonard, H. B., Epstein M. J., and Goodwin, T. F. "AARP Foundation (A) & (B)." *Harvard Business School* (A—Case #107–051) (B—Case #107–052), 2007.

Kaplan, R. S. "New Profit Inc.: Governing the Nonprofit Enterprise," *Harvard Business School* (Case #100–052), 2001.

Kaplan, R. S. "Boston Lyric Opera," *Harvard Business School* (Case #101–111), 2001.

Leonard, H. B., Epstein, M. J., and Smith, W. "Digital Divide Data: A Social Enterprise in Action." *Harvard Business School* (Case #307–106), 2007.

Leonard, H. B., Epstein, M. J., and Tritter, M. "The Augusta National Golf Club Controversy (A) (B) & (C)." *Harvard Business School* (Case #306–029), 2005.

Leonard, H. B., Epstein, M. J., and Tritter, M. "Opportunity International: Measurement and Mission." *Harvard Business School* (Case #307–067), 2007.

Leonard, H. B., Epstein, M. J., and Tritter, M. "Absolute Return for Kids." *Harvard Business School* (Case #309–036), 2008.

Leonard, H. B., Epstein, M. J., and Winig, L. "Playgrounds and Performance: Results Management at KaBOOM! (A)." *Harvard Business School* (Case #306–031), 2005.

McFarlan, F. W., Leonard, H. B., and Tritter, M. "Dana Hall: Funding a Mission (A) (B) & (C)." *Harvard Business School* (A—Case #306–090) (B—Case #306–100) (C—Case #306–106), 2007.

McFarlan, F. W., and Elias, J. "Trinity College (A) (B) & (C)." *Harvard Business School*, (A—Case #397–068) (B—Case #397–069) (C—Case #397–070), 1997.

McFarlan, F. W., and Elias, J. "Mt. Auburn Hospital." *Harvard Business School* (Case #397–083), 1997.

McFarlan, F. W., and Vargas, I. "Harold Morton and the Riverdale Board (A) & (B)." *Harvard Business School* (A—Case #303–114) (B—Case #303–115), 2003.

McFarlan, F. W., and Vitali, M. R. "From Little Things Big Things Grow: The Clontarf Foundation Program for Aboriginal Boys." *Harvard Business School* (Case #910–402), 2009.

Roberts, L. M., and Kanji, A. "Jeanette Clough at Mt. Auburn Hospital." *Harvard Business School* (Case #406–068), 2005.

Wei-Skillern, J., and Herman, K. "Habitat for Humanity—Egypt." *Harvard Business School* (Case #307–001), 2006.

The Authors

Marc J. Epstein is Distinguished Research Professor of Management at Jones Graduate School of Business at Rice University in Houston, Texas. Prior to joining Rice, Dr. Epstein was a professor at Stanford Business School, Harvard Business School, and INSEAD (European Institute of Business Administration). In both academic research and managerial practice, Dr. Epstein has extensively worked in the areas of sustainability, governance, performance measurement, and accountability in both corporations and nonprofit organizations.

Dr. Epstein has also focused on the measurement of corporate social, environmental, and economic impacts for most of his career. He is also currently working on microfinance, entrepreneurship in developing countries, education and technology in developing countries, and nonprofit performance measurement and governance.

His twenty authored or coauthored books and over one hundred professional articles include many award-winners, including *Making Innovation Work: How to Manage It, Measure It, and Profit from It* and *Counting What Counts: Turning Corporate Accountability to Competitive Advantage.* His most recent book, *Making Sustainability Work: Best Practices in Managing and Measuring Corporate Social, Environmental, and Economic Impacts,* was released in 2008.

F. Warren McFarlan has been a member of the Harvard Graduate School of Business Administration faculty since 1964.

Former chairman of Harvard's Advanced Management Program, he also served as senior associate dean from 1990 to 2004. In this position he had a number of roles including five years as head of External Relations from 1995 to 2000. He is currently the Albert H. Gordon Professor of Business Administration Emeritus. He has worked and published extensively in the field of IT, authoring or coauthoring thirteen books and over 150 cases and numerous articles in the *Harvard Business Review* and elsewhere. *Corporate Information Strategy and Management: Text and Cases* (seventh edition), coauthored with Professors Lynda M. Applegate and Robert D. Austin, appeared in 2006.

For the past decade, he has been associated with the HBS Social Enterprise Initiative, teaching in a number of its executive programs. He has served continuously for over thirty years on both corporate and nonprofit boards in the United States and abroad, and has written a number of articles and cases in the area of social enterprise.

Index

Page numbers in italic refer to exhibits, figures, or tables.